Entrepreneurship: A Very Short Introduction

VERY SHORT INTRODUCTIONS are for anyone wanting a stimulating and accessible way in to a new subject. They are written by experts, and have been published in more than 40 languages worldwide.

The series began in 1995, and now represents a wide variety of topics in history, philosophy, religion, science, and the humanities. The VSI library now contains nearly 400 volumes—a Very Short Introduction to everything from ancient Egypt and Indian philosophy to conceptual art and cosmology—and will continue to grow in a variety of disciplines.

Very Short Introductions available now:

ADVERTISING Winston Fletcher
AFRICAN HISTORY John Parker and
    Richard Rathbone
AGNOSTICISM Robin Le Poidevin
AMERICAN HISTORY Paul S. Boyer
AMERICAN IMMIGRATION
    David A. Gerber
AMERICAN POLITICAL PARTIES
    AND ELECTIONS L. Sandy Maisel
AMERICAN POLITICS
    Richard M. Valelly
THE AMERICAN
    PRESIDENCY Charles O. Jones
ANAESTHESIA Aidan O'Donnell
ANARCHISM Colin Ward
ANCIENT EGYPT Ian Shaw
ANCIENT GREECE Paul Cartledge
ANCIENT PHILOSOPHY Julia Annas
ANCIENT WARFARE Harry Sidebottom
ANGELS David Albert Jones
ANGLICANISM Mark Chapman
THE ANGLO-SAXON AGE John Blair
THE ANIMAL KINGDOM
    Peter Holland
ANIMAL RIGHTS David DeGrazia
THE ANTARCTIC Klaus Dodds
ANTISEMITISM Steven Beller
ANXIETY Daniel Freeman and
    Jason Freeman
THE APOCRYPHAL GOSPELS
    Paul Foster
ARCHAEOLOGY Paul Bahn
ARCHITECTURE Andrew Ballantyne
ARISTOCRACY William Doyle
ARISTOTLE Jonathan Barnes

ART HISTORY Dana Arnold
ART THEORY Cynthia Freeland
ASTROBIOLOGY David C. Catling
ATHEISM Julian Baggini
AUGUSTINE Henry Chadwick
AUSTRALIA Kenneth Morgan
AUTISM Uta Frith
THE AVANT GARDE
    David Cottington
THE AZTECS David Carrasco
BACTERIA Sebastian G. B. Amyes
BARTHES Jonathan Culler
THE BEATS David Sterritt
BEAUTY Roger Scruton
BESTSELLERS John Sutherland
THE BIBLE John Riches
BIBLICAL ARCHAEOLOGY
    Eric H. Cline
BIOGRAPHY Hermione Lee
THE BLUES Elijah Wald
THE BOOK OF MORMON
    Terryl Givens
BORDERS Alexander C. Diener and
    Joshua Hagen
THE BRAIN Michael O'Shea
THE BRITISH CONSTITUTION
    Martin Loughlin
THE BRITISH EMPIRE Ashley Jackson
BRITISH POLITICS Anthony Wright
BUDDHA Michael Carrithers
BUDDHISM Damien Keown
BUDDHIST ETHICS Damien Keown
CANCER Nicholas James
CAPITALISM James Fulcher
CATHOLICISM Gerald O'Collins

CAUSATION Stephen Mumford and
    Rani Lill Anjum
THE CELL Terence Allen and
    Graham Cowling
THE CELTS Barry Cunliffe
CHAOS Leonard Smith
CHILDREN'S LITERATURE
    Kimberley Reynolds
CHINESE LITERATURE Sabina Knight
CHOICE THEORY Michael Allingham
CHRISTIAN ART Beth Williamson
CHRISTIAN ETHICS D. Stephen Long
CHRISTIANITY Linda Woodhead
CITIZENSHIP Richard Bellamy
CIVIL ENGINEERING David Muir Wood
CLASSICAL MYTHOLOGY
    Helen Morales
CLASSICS Mary Beard and
    John Henderson
CLAUSEWITZ Michael Howard
CLIMATE Mark Maslin
THE COLD WAR Robert McMahon
COLONIAL AMERICA Alan Taylor
COLONIAL LATIN AMERICAN
    LITERATURE Rolena Adorno
COMEDY Matthew Bevis
COMMUNISM Leslie Holmes
THE COMPUTER Darrel Ince
THE CONQUISTADORS Matthew
    Restall and Felipe Fernández-Armesto
CONSCIENCE Paul Strohm
CONSCIOUSNESS Susan Blackmore
CONTEMPORARY ART
    Julian Stallabrass
CONTEMPORARY FICTION
    Robert Eaglestone
CONTINENTAL PHILOSOPHY
    Simon Critchley
COSMOLOGY Peter Coles
CRITICAL THEORY Stephen Eric Bronner
THE CRUSADES Christopher Tyerman
CRYPTOGRAPHY Fred Piper and
    Sean Murphy
THE CULTURAL REVOLUTION
    Richard Curt Kraus
DADA AND SURREALISM
    David Hopkins
DARWIN Jonathan Howard
THE DEAD SEA SCROLLS Timothy Lim
DEMOCRACY Bernard Crick
DERRIDA Simon Glendinning
DESCARTES Tom Sorell
DESERTS Nick Middleton
DESIGN John Heskett
DEVELOPMENTAL BIOLOGY
    Lewis Wolpert
THE DEVIL Darren Oldridge
DIASPORA KEVIN KENNY
DICTIONARIES Lynda Mugglestone
DINOSAURS David Norman
DIPLOMACY Joseph M. Siracusa
DOCUMENTARY FILM Patricia
    Aufderheide
DREAMING J. Allan Hobson
DRUGS Leslie Iversen
DRUIDS Barry Cunliffe
EARLY MUSIC Thomas Forrest Kelly
THE EARTH Martin Redfern
ECONOMICS Partha Dasgupta
EDUCATION Gary Thomas
EGYPTIAN MYTH Geraldine Pinch
EIGHTEENTH-CENTURY BRITAIN
    Paul Langford
THE ELEMENTS Philip Ball
EMOTION Dylan Evans
EMPIRE Stephen Howe
ENGELS Terrell Carver
ENGINEERING David Blockley
ENGLISH LITERATURE Jonathan Bate
ENTREPRENEURSHIP Paul Westhead
    and Mike Wright
ENVIRONMENTAL ECONOMICS
    Stephen Smith
EPIDEMIOLOGY Rodolfo Saracci
ETHICS Simon Blackburn
THE EUROPEAN UNION John Pinder
    and Simon Usherwood
EVOLUTION Brian and Deborah
    Charlesworth
EXISTENTIALISM Thomas Flynn
FASCISM Kevin Passmore
FASHION Rebecca Arnold
FEMINISM Margaret Walters
FILM Michael Wood
FILM MUSIC Kathryn Kalinak
THE FIRST WORLD WAR
    Michael Howard
FOLK MUSIC Mark Slobin
FOOD John Krebs
FORENSIC PSYCHOLOGY David Canter
FORENSIC SCIENCE Jim Fraser
FOSSILS Keith Thomson

FOUCAULT Gary Gutting
FRACTALS Kenneth Falconer
FREE SPEECH Nigel Warburton
FREE WILL Thomas Pink
FRENCH LITERATURE John D. Lyons
THE FRENCH REVOLUTION
    William Doyle
FREUD Anthony Storr
FUNDAMENTALISM Malise Ruthven
GALAXIES John Gribbin
GALILEO Stillman Drake
GAME THEORY Ken Binmore
GANDHI Bhikhu Parekh
GENIUS Andrew Robinson
GEOGRAPHY John Matthews and
    David Herbert
GEOPOLITICS Klaus Dodds
GERMAN LITERATURE Nicholas Boyle
GERMAN PHILOSOPHY Andrew Bowie
GLOBAL CATASTROPHES Bill McGuire
GLOBAL ECONOMIC HISTORY
    Robert C. Allen
GLOBAL WARMING Mark Maslin
GLOBALIZATION Manfred Steger
THE GOTHIC Nick Groom
GOVERNANCE Mark Bevir
THE GREAT DEPRESSION AND THE
    NEW DEAL Eric Rauchway
HABERMAS James Gordon Finlayson
HAPPINESS Daniel M. Haybron
HEGEL Peter Singer
HEIDEGGER Michael Inwood
HERODOTUS Jennifer T. Roberts
HIEROGLYPHS Penelope Wilson
HINDUISM Kim Knott
HISTORY John H. Arnold
THE HISTORY OF ASTRONOMY
    Michael Hoskin
THE HISTORY OF LIFE Michael Benton
THE HISTORY OF
    MATHEMATICS Jacqueline Stedall
THE HISTORY OF
    MEDICINE William Bynum
THE HISTORY OF TIME
    Leofranc Holford-Strevens
HIV/AIDS Alan Whiteside
HOBBES Richard Tuck
HUMAN EVOLUTION Bernard Wood
HUMAN RIGHTS Andrew Clapham
HUMANISM Stephen Law
HUME A. J. Ayer

IDEOLOGY Michael Freeden
INDIAN PHILOSOPHY Sue Hamilton
INFORMATION Luciano Floridi
INNOVATION Mark Dodgson and
    David Gann
INTELLIGENCE Ian J. Deary
INTERNATIONAL
    MIGRATION Khalid Koser
INTERNATIONAL RELATIONS
    Paul Wilkinson
INTERNATIONAL SECURITY
    Christopher S. Browning
ISLAM Malise Ruthven
ISLAMIC HISTORY Adam Silverstein
ITALIAN LITERATURE Peter
    Hainsworth and David Robey
JESUS Richard Bauckham
JOURNALISM Ian Hargreaves
JUDAISM Norman Solomon
JUNG Anthony Stevens
KABBALAH Joseph Dan
KAFKA Ritchie Robertson
KANT Roger Scruton
KEYNES Robert Skidelsky
KIERKEGAARD Patrick Gardiner
THE KORAN Michael Cook
LANDSCAPES AND
    GEOMORPHOLOGY
    Andrew Goudie and Heather Viles
LANGUAGES Stephen R. Anderson
LATE ANTIQUITY Gillian Clark
LAW Raymond Wacks
THE LAWS OF THERMODYNAMICS
    Peter Atkins
LEADERSHIP Keith Grint
LINCOLN Allen C. Guelzo
LINGUISTICS Peter Matthews
LITERARY THEORY Jonathan Culler
LOCKE John Dunn
LOGIC Graham Priest
MACHIAVELLI Quentin Skinner
MADNESS Andrew Scull
MAGIC Owen Davies
MAGNA CARTA Nicholas Vincent
MAGNETISM Stephen Blundell
MALTHUS Donald Winch
MANAGEMENT John Hendry
MAO Delia Davin
MARINE BIOLOGY Philip V. Mladenov
THE MARQUIS DE SADE John Phillips
MARTIN LUTHER Scott H. Hendrix

MARTYRDOM Jolyon Mitchell
MARX Peter Singer
MATHEMATICS Timothy Gowers
THE MEANING OF LIFE Terry Eagleton
MEDICAL ETHICS Tony Hope
MEDICAL LAW Charles Foster
MEDIEVAL BRITAIN John Gillingham
and Ralph A. Griffiths
MEMORY Jonathan K. Foster
METAPHYSICS Stephen Mumford
MICHAEL FARADAY Frank A.J.L. James
MODERN ART David Cottington
MODERN CHINA Rana Mitter
MODERN FRANCE Vanessa R. Schwartz
MODERN IRELAND Senia Pašeta
MODERN JAPAN
Christopher Goto-Jones
MODERN LATIN AMERICAN
LITERATURE
Roberto González Echevarría
MODERN WAR Richard English
MODERNISM Christopher Butler
MOLECULES Philip Ball
THE MONGOLS Morris Rossabi
MORMONISM Richard Lyman Bushman
MUHAMMAD Jonathan A.C. Brown
MULTICULTURALISM Ali Rattansi
MUSIC Nicholas Cook
MYTH Robert A. Segal
THE NAPOLEONIC WARS Mike Rapport
NATIONALISM Steven Grosby
NELSON MANDELA Elleke Boehmer
NEOLIBERALISM Manfred Steger and
Ravi Roy
NETWORKS Guido Caldarelli and
Michele Catanzaro
THE NEW TESTAMENT Luke Timothy
Johnson
THE NEW TESTAMENT AS
LITERATURE Kyle Keefer
NEWTON Robert Iliffe
NIETZSCHE Michael Tanner
NINETEENTH-CENTURY
BRITAIN Christopher Harvie and
H. C. G. Matthew
THE NORMAN CONQUEST
George Garnett
NORTH AMERICAN INDIANS
Theda Perdue and Michael D. Green
NORTHERN IRELAND
Marc Mulholland

NOTHING Frank Close
NUCLEAR POWER Maxwell Irvine
NUCLEAR WEAPONS
Joseph M. Siracusa
NUMBERS Peter M. Higgins
OBJECTIVITY Stephen Gaukroger
THE OLD TESTAMENT
Michael D. Coogan
THE ORCHESTRA D. Kern Holoman
ORGANIZATIONS Mary Jo Hatch
PAGANISM Owen Davies
THE PALESTINIAN-ISRAELI
CONFLICT Martin Bunton
PARTICLE PHYSICS Frank Close
PAUL E. P. Sanders
PENTECOSTALISM William K. Kay
THE PERIODIC TABLE Eric R. Scerri
PHILOSOPHY Edward Craig
PHILOSOPHY OF LAW Raymond Wacks
PHILOSOPHY OF SCIENCE
Samir Okasha
PHOTOGRAPHY Steve Edwards
PLAGUE Paul Slack
PLANETS David A. Rothery
PLANTS Timothy Walker
PLATO Julia Annas
POLITICAL PHILOSOPHY David Miller
POLITICS Kenneth Minogue
POSTCOLONIALISM Robert Young
POSTMODERNISM Christopher Butler
POSTSTRUCTURALISM
Catherine Belsey
PREHISTORY Chris Gosden
PRESOCRATIC PHILOSOPHY
Catherine Osborne
PRIVACY Raymond Wacks
PROBABILITY John Haigh
PROGRESSIVISM Walter Nugent
PROTESTANTISM Mark A. Noll
PSYCHIATRY Tom Burns
PSYCHOLOGY Gillian Butler and
Freda McManus
PURITANISM Francis J. Bremer
THE QUAKERS Pink Dandelion
QUANTUM THEORY
John Polkinghorne
RACISM Ali Rattansi
RADIOACTIVITY Claudio Tuniz
RASTAFARI Ennis B. Edmonds
THE REAGAN REVOLUTION
Gil Troy

REALITY Jan Westerhoff
THE REFORMATION Peter Marshall
RELATIVITY Russell Stannard
RELIGION IN AMERICA Timothy Beal
THE RENAISSANCE Jerry Brotton
RENAISSANCE ART Geraldine A. Johnson
RHETORIC Richard Toye
RISK Baruch Fischhoff and John Kadvany
RIVERS Nick Middleton
ROBOTICS Alan Winfield
ROMAN BRITAIN Peter Salway
THE ROMAN EMPIRE
    Christopher Kelly
THE ROMAN REPUBLIC
    David M. Gwynn
ROMANTICISM Michael Ferber
ROUSSEAU Robert Wokler
RUSSELL A. C. Grayling
RUSSIAN HISTORY Geoffrey Hosking
RUSSIAN LITERATURE Catriona Kelly
THE RUSSIAN REVOLUTION
    S. A. Smith
SCHIZOPHRENIA Chris Frith and
    Eve Johnstone
SCHOPENHAUER Christopher Janaway
SCIENCE AND RELIGION Thomas Dixon
SCIENCE FICTION David Seed
THE SCIENTIFIC REVOLUTION
    Lawrence M. Principe
SCOTLAND Rab Houston
SEXUALITY Véronique Mottier
SHAKESPEARE Germaine Greer
SIKHISM Eleanor Nesbitt
THE SILK ROAD James A. Millward
SLEEP Steven W. Lockley and
    Russell G. Foster
SOCIAL AND CULTURAL
    ANTHROPOLOGY
    John Monaghan and Peter Just
SOCIALISM Michael Newman
SOCIOLINGUISTICS John Edwards

SOCIOLOGY Steve Bruce
SOCRATES C. C. W. Taylor
THE SOVIET UNION Stephen Lovell
THE SPANISH CIVIL WAR
    Helen Graham
SPANISH LITERATURE Jo Labanyi
SPINOZA Roger Scruton
SPIRITUALITY Philip Sheldrake
STARS Andrew King
STATISTICS David J. Hand
STEM CELLS Jonathan Slack
STUART BRITAIN John Morrill
SUPERCONDUCTIVITY Stephen Blundell
SYMMETRY Ian Stewart
TERRORISM Charles Townshend
THEOLOGY David F. Ford
THOMAS AQUINAS Fergus Kerr
THOUGHT Tim Bayne
TOCQUEVILLE Harvey C. Mansfield
TRAGEDY Adrian Poole
THE TROJAN WAR Eric H. Cline
TRUST Katherine Hawley
THE TUDORS John Guy
TWENTIETH-CENTURY BRITAIN
    Kenneth O. Morgan
THE UNITED NATIONS Jussi M.
    Hanhimäki
THE U.S. CONGRESS Donald A. Ritchie
THE U.S. SUPREME COURT Linda
    Greenhouse
UTOPIANISM Lyman Tower Sargent
THE VIKINGS Julian Richards
VIRUSES Dorothy H. Crawford
WITCHCRAFT Malcolm Gaskill
WITTGENSTEIN A. C. Grayling
WORK Stephen Fineman
WORLD MUSIC Philip Bohlman
THE WORLD TRADE
    ORGANIZATION Amrita Narlikar
WRITING AND SCRIPT Andrew
    Robinson

Available soon:

BLACK HOLES Katherine Blundell
HUMOUR Noël Carroll
AMERICAN LEGAL HISTORY
    G. Edward White

REVOLUTIONS Jack A. Gladstone
FAMILY LAW Jonathan Herring

For more information visit our website
www.oup.com/vsi/

Paul Westhead and Mike Wright

ENTREPRENEURSHIP

A Very Short Introduction

OXFORD
UNIVERSITY PRESS

OXFORD
UNIVERSITY PRESS

Great Clarendon Street, Oxford, ox2 6DP,
United Kingdom

Oxford University Press is a department of the University of Oxford.
It furthers the University's objective of excellence in research, scholarship,
and education by publishing worldwide. Oxford is a registered trade mark of
Oxford University Press in the UK and in certain other countries

© Paul Westhead and Mike Wright 2013

The moral rights of the authors have been asserted

First Edition published in 2013
Impression: 1

Published in the United States of America by Oxford University Press
198 Madison Avenue, New York, NY 10016, United States of America

British Library Cataloguing in Publication Data
Data available

Library of Congress Control Number: 2013942448

ISBN 978-0-19-967054-3

Printed in Great Britain by
Ashford Colour Press Ltd, Gosport, Hampshire

For Benjamin, Julien, and Stephanie

Contents

Acknowledgements xiii

List of illustrations xv

List of tables xvii

1 The importance of entrepreneurship 1

2 Discovering and creating opportunities 21

3 Exploiting opportunities 38

4 Entrepreneurs' context 54

5 Entrepreneurial thinking and learning 79

6 Forms of entrepreneurial venture 98

7 The future 125

Further reading 137

Index 149

Acknowledgements

Thanks to Stephanie Wright, the anonymous reviewers, and the editors for their comments on an earlier draft.

List of illustrations

1 Themes explored in entrepreneurship studies **9**

2 Renovo share price **40**

3 Input–process–output model of strategic entrepreneurship **45**
   From Hitt M. A., et al, Strategic Entrepreneurship: Creating Value for Individuals, Organization, and Society. *Academy of Management Perspectives* (2011)

4 Resource orchestration **47**

5 Overall entrepreneurship rates between countries 2011 **62**
   From Kelley D., Singer S., and Herrington M. (2012). *2011 Global Entrepreneurship Monitor Executive Report*. London: Global Entrepreneurship Research Association (GERA)

6 Conceptualized types of family firm **104**

List of tables

1 Summary of approaches for describing the entrepreneur as an individual **7**

Adapted from Cunningham, J. B. and Lischeron, J. (1991). Defining Entrepreneurship. *Journal of Small Business Management*, 29(1): 45–61

2 Entrepreneurial firms: positive economic and non-economic contributions and barriers to enterprise **12**

3 Types of government support for new firm formation and development **17**

Adapted from Storey, D. J. (1994). *Understanding the Small Business Sector*. London, Thomson Learning

4 Opportunity discovery versus opportunity creation **27**

© 2007. Strategic Management Society. Published by John Wiley & Sons, Ltd

5 Causation and effectuation views on the source of opportunity **32**

Adapted from Read, S., Sarasvathy, S., Dew, N., Wiltbank, R., and Ohlsson, A. (2011) *Effectual Entrepreneurship*. New York: Routledge

6 Links between effectuation process steps and bricolage actions **36**

7 Elements of a business plan **52**

8 Views on new small business development and the individual **56**

Adapted from Gibb, A. and Ritchie, J. (1982). Understanding the Process of Starting Small Businesses. *European Small Business Journal*, 1(1): 26–45

9 Influences on the development of entrepreneurial ideas and ambitions at different stages of life **57**

Adapted from Gibb A., Enterprise Culture – ID Meaning and Implications for Education and Training (1987). *Journal of European Industrial Training*

10 Regional variations in new firm formation rates across seven European Community countries **60**

Adapted from Reynolds, P., Storey, D. J., and Westhead, P. (1994). Cross-National Comparisons of the Variation in New Firm Formation Rates. *Regional Studies*, 28(4): 443–456

11 Smith's profiles of craftsman and opportunist entrepreneurs **63**

12 Categorization of habitual entrepreneurship **66**

13 Main hurdles reported at work by women **70**

From Kariv, D. (2013). *Female Entrepreneurship and the New Venture Creation: An International Perspective*. London: Routledge

14 'Micro and macro perspectives and female entrepreneurship **73**

From Kariv, D. (2013). *Female Entrepreneurship and the New Venture Creation: An International Perspective*. London: Routledge

15 Personality trait dimensions in entrepreneurship studies **80**

16 Cognitive heuristics and biases in entrepreneurship **89**

17 Advantages and disadvantages of family firms **100**

18 Barriers to succession planning in family firms **102**

Adapted from Kets de Vries. (1993). The dynamics of family controlled firms: The good and the bad news. *Organizational Dynamics*, 21(2): 13

19 Corporate entrepreneurship terminology **106**

Adapted from Sharma P. and Chrisman J. J. (1999). Toward a Reconciliation of the Definitional Issues in the Field of Corporate Entrepreneurship. *Entrepreneurship Theory and Practice*, 23(3): 11–27

20 Corporate entrepreneurship (CE) attributes **108**

Adapted from Covin J. and Miles M. (1999). Corporate Entrepreneurship and the Pursuit of Competitive Advantage. *Entrepreneurship Theory and Practice*, 23(3): 47–63

21 Typology of buyouts **111**

22 Types of academic spin-off firm **117**

The publisher and authors apologize for any errors or omissions in the above list. If contacted they will be happy to rectify these at the earliest opportunity.

Chapter 1
The importance of entrepreneurship

We appear to be living in a golden age for entrepreneurship. In 2011, a Global Entrepreneurship Monitor (GEM) survey of more than 140,000 adults (18–64 years of age) in fifty-four economies estimated that 388 million entrepreneurs were actively engaged in starting and running new businesses. Entrepreneurs can be vital agents of innovative change whose actions lead to the creation of new firms. They can also transform existing firms to exploit economic and socially beneficial opportunities. In the popular media, entrepreneurs are often presented playing a key role in promoting economic development. Indeed, GEM studies have discovered a significant link between the rate of entrepreneurial activity in a country and growth in that country's gross domestic product (GDP), although the link is not consistent across all countries. Entrepreneurs and their businesses can generate wealth and jobs, which can enable social and regional inequality to be reduced. Entrepreneurs can be pulled into entrepreneurship because they want to exploit a perceived business opportunity, or pushed into it of necessity because they have no other options for work. Either way, they are increasingly seen as the panacea to solve national and local development issues.

The expectation that entrepreneurs can provide the panacea to economic ills may be an unrealistic one. Joseph Schumpeter warned that while entrepreneurial acts 'create' new sources of competitive advantage, products and services, firms, industries, jobs, and wealth, at the same time they also 'destroy' firms and jobs in now out-of-date activities. In the popular mindset entrepreneurs are often portrayed as heroic yet maverick individuals, single-handedly and relentlessly pursuing opportunity and enjoying exotic lifestyles as a result. The dominant popular entrepreneur image relates to a Western heroic white male figure exhibiting aggression and assertiveness to create or discover business opportunities. But, when businesses close, with people losing their jobs and nefarious activities being revealed, some of the same entrepreneurs are then castigated as villains (e.g. Conrad Black, Robert Maxwell, Asil Nadir). So entrepreneurs can be heroes and villains, sometimes both at the same time depending on your point of view. Books about Richard Branson, for example, have presented conflicting portraits ranging from adventurous global entrepreneur to cunning and ruthless operator with a knack for undermining his rivals.

Because of the widely held belief about the contribution of entrepreneurs to the generation of economic and social well-being, international agencies and governments worldwide are promoting entrepreneurship policies. Venture capital (VC) firms operate to fund entrepreneurs in the belief that they can generate high financial returns. National research bodies, universities, and specialized research centres, as well as research foundations, have been keen to support research based on the assumption that this will help further the role of entrepreneurship in invigorating economic, technological, and social progress.

Entrepreneurs have been catapulted into the consciousness of the wider media through their high-profile activities, which help change fundamentally the rules of the game in a market. For example, Stelios Haji-Ioannou and easyJet transformed the airline industry in Europe, James Dyson's bagless cleaner changed the vacuum cleaner market, and Bill Gates's Microsoft and Steve

Jobs's Apple, in their different ways, transformed the personal computing, communications, and entertainment markets.

Prime-time television programmes showing entrepreneurs and inventors pitching their ideas to rich investors have helped popularize entrepreneurs to a wide audience. Originating in Japan, this concept has itself proved to be highly entrepreneurial. Entrepreneurship-related shows are shown worldwide under different names, such as *Shark Tank* in the United States, *Dragons' Den* in the UK, and *Fikr wa Talash* in Afghanistan. But not apparently in France where, according to the apocryphal (but untrue) statement attributed to President George W. Bush, the French do not have a word for entrepreneur.

The number of scholars researching entrepreneurship has grown rapidly. Academy of Management Entrepreneurship Division membership has increased by almost two and a half times, to top 2,750, in the decade from 2001 to 2011. Business schools report a proliferation of entrepreneurship courses at undergraduate and postgraduate levels. Science, technology, engineering, and medical departments in universities have also introduced entrepreneurship courses for students and faculty who want to create businesses to exploit the inventions they have created in the laboratory. Secondary and primary schools are now teaching entrepreneurship. These courses discuss hands-on issues relating to the creation of private and, increasingly, social ventures, as well examining how existing, large, and family organizations can be entrepreneurial. In addition, courses illustrate theoretical and policy issues.

Some students have made significant wealth from their new ventures. Alex Tew conceived The Million Dollar Homepage to raise money for his university education. The home page consisted of a million pixels arranged in a 1,000 × 1,000 pixel grid. The image-based links on it were sold for US$1 per pixel in 10 × 10 blocks. The purchasers of these pixel blocks provided tiny images

3

to be displayed on them, a uniform resource locator (URL) to which the images were linked, and a slogan to be displayed when hovering a cursor over the link. The aim of the website was to sell all of the pixels in the image. With the last 1,000 pixels being put up for auction on eBay, a final total of $1,037,100 was grossed.

Other students have dropped out to pursue major entrepreneurial ideas that have germinated at college. Mark Zuckerberg famously dropped out of Harvard in his sophomore year to complete the Facebook project, which he launched from his dormitory room.

Despite growing interest and activity relating to the entrepreneurship phenomenon, considerable debate surrounds the notion of entrepreneurs and entrepreneurship. Entrepreneurship and entrepreneurs are complicated and ambiguous phenomena. In this *Very Short Introduction*, our aim is to reflect this complexity and ambiguity, but also to weave a pathway through the debate and offer some clarity to the reader.

We provide a guide to entrepreneurial events, processes, and outputs in the contexts in which they occur. We will explore the following questions: What is entrepreneurship and why is it important? What do entrepreneurs do? Where do entrepreneurs come from? Do some types of entrepreneurs make greater contributions? What is distinctive about entrepreneurs? How do entrepreneurs think and learn from their experiences? What is the array of organizational modes in which entrepreneurship takes place?

Entrepreneurship

Entrepreneurship is about what entrepreneurs do. 'Entrepreneur' is a French word first appearing in the 1437 *Dictionnaire de la langue française*. Three definitions were listed in the dictionary, with the most common meaning referring to 'a person who is active and achieves something'. The verb

4

'entreprendre' means 'to undertake something'. At the beginning of the 17th century, an entrepreneur in France was viewed as 'a person who takes risks,' but not all people who undertook risks were considered entrepreneurs. During the 18th century, a person who was contracted to perform a certain large task, generally for the state, for a fixed price was regarded as an entrepreneur.

Until the 18th century, there was no equivalent to the French 'entrepreneur' concept in the English language. A *Dictionary of the English Language* from 1755 reported the following definition: 'Adventurer, he that seeks occasion of hazard; he that puts himself in the hand of chance'. Over time, the concept of entrepreneur in English became more broadly defined, and related to 'situations where one person engaged in projects involving risk where the profit was uncertain'. By the end of the 18th century, the undertaker concept was replaced by the capitalist concept of a businessman.

Today, there continues to be no agreed definition of entrepreneurs and entrepreneurship. The Organisation for Economic Co-operation and Development (OECD) adopts a broad definition where entrepreneurship appears in both some small and large firms, in some new firms and established family firms, in private firms focusing on profit and social enterprises seeking to generate broader social and environmental benefits, in the formal and informal economy, in legal and illegal activities, in innovative and more conventional concerns, and in all regions and economic sub-sectors.

Entrepreneurs' roles

Economic, sociological, personality/traits, psychodynamic, and/or cognitive approaches have been used to explain what entrepreneurs do. We shall explore these approaches later on, but this diversity and lack of consensus is illustrated by the following roles identified over two and a half centuries of research. The entrepreneur is:

1. a person who assumes the risk associated with uncertainty;
2. a person who supplies financial capital;
3. an opportunity creator and innovator;
4. a decision-maker;
5. an industrial leader;
6. a manager or superintendent;
7. an organizer and coordinator of economic resources;
8. the owner of an enterprise;
9. an employer of factors of production;
10. a contractor;
11. an arbitrageur;
12. an allocator of resources among alternative uses;
13. a channel for the spillover of knowledge from a knowledge organization into a new firm to exploit the knowledge;
14. an alert discoverer or seeker of opportunities.

Approaches to describe the entrepreneur

Roles of entrepreneurs have primarily emanated from economics' focus on the functions of the entrepreneur in the market. Recently, more behaviourally oriented approaches have focused on the characteristics of the individual carrying out these roles, specifically 'who is the entrepreneur'. Diversity in approaches to describe the entrepreneur as an individual is summarized in Table 1, where a distinction can be made between the great person school, psychological characteristics school, classical school, management school, leadership school, and the intrapreneurship school approaches.

The entrepreneurial process

The entrepreneurial process is at the epicenter of the debate about entrepreneurship. This is because it concerns what needs to take place to make entrepreneurship happen. Lack of consensus about

Table 1. Summary of approaches for describing the entrepreneur as an individual

Entrepreneurial model	Central focus or purpose	Assumption	Skills and behaviour	Situation
Great person school	Born with intuitive ability	'Inborn' intuition makes the entrepreneur different	Intuition, vigour, energy, persistence, and self-esteem	Start-up
Psychological characteristics school	Unique values, attitudes, and needs that drive them	Values shape behaviour to satisfy needs	Personal values, risk taking; need for achievement, etc.	Start-up
Classical school	Focus on innovation	Process of doing rather than owning	Innovation, creativity, and discovery	Start-up and early growth
Management school	Organizers that own, manage, and assume risk	Can develop and train	Production planning, people organizing, capitalization, and budgeting	Early growth and maturity
Leadership school	Leaders that adapt their style to the needs of people	Cannot accomplish a goal on their own	Motivating, directing and leading	Early growth and maturity
Intrapreneurship school	Entrepreneurial skills used in complex organizations	Adaptation and organization building	Alertness to opportunities and maximizing decisions	Maturity and change

Source: Adapted from Cunningham and Lischeron (1991: 47)

7

'what entrepreneurs do' and 'who entrepreneurs are' gives rise to several approaches to understanding entrepreneurs and the entrepreneurial process. Generally, the entrepreneurial process involves all the functions and activities associated with perceiving opportunities and pursuing them. A narrow view focuses on the emergence of new organizations, while a broader view focuses on the emergence of opportunities irrespective of whether it takes place in a new or existing firm. Accessing resources is key. Some see entrepreneurship as the process by which individuals pursue and exploit opportunities irrespective of the resources they currently control. Others focus on how entrepreneurs can utilize the resource they have to hand, while yet others examine the process by which entrepreneurs access and coordinate their resources.

Organizing framework

Bill Gartner's framework for describing the phenomenon of new venture creation integrated four major perspectives in entrepreneurship. He made a distinction between: the characteristics of the individual(s) starting the new venture; the organization they create; the environment surrounding the new venture; and the process by which the new venture is created. Building on these insights, six themes within entrepreneurship studies are highlighted in Figure 1.

Theme 1 relates to *theory*. Several theories explore the entrepreneurial process, and the behaviour and performance of entrepreneurs and their organizations. These theories reflect the diversity of the nature of entrepreneurship and entrepreneurs.

Theme 2 relates to the *external environment for entrepreneurship*. To generate economic and non-economic benefits, governments in developed and developing economies have introduced policies to address external environmental barriers to business formation

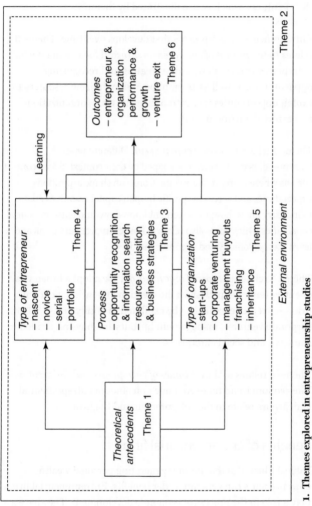

1. Themes explored in entrepreneurship studies

External environment (Theme 2)

Theoretical antecedents
Theme 1

Type of entrepreneur
– nascent
– novice
– serial
– portfolio
Theme 4

Process
– opportunity recognition
 & information search
– resource acquisition
 & business strategies
Theme 3

Type of organization
– start-ups
– corporate venturing
– management buyouts
– franchising
– inheritance
Theme 5

Outcomes
– entrepreneur &
 organization
– performance &
 growth
– venture exit
Theme 6

Learning

and development. These contexts shape resource availability, the actions undertaken by entrepreneurs, and the performance of their ventures, which is also illustrated by theme 4.

Entrepreneurship is a process that develops over time. Theme 3 relates to the *process of entrepreneurship* and focuses upon what entrepreneurs do with regard to creating and recognizing opportunities, as well as assembling and mobilizing resources to exploit opportunities (i.e. entrepreneurial team, organizational, and external environmental).

Theme 4 relates to *types of entrepreneur*. Different types of entrepreneurs exist and can be shaped by their context. Social context, such as where entrepreneurs come from, can shape aspirations, expectations, and access to specific human capital resources relating to industry know-how, management know-how, and entrepreneurial capabilities. Differences also relate to how entrepreneurs think and learn (i.e. personality and cognitive mindset).

Theme 5 relates to *types of organization*. We adopt a broad view of entrepreneurship. Besides the creation of new independent firms, entrepreneurship can be exhibited in family firms, corporate ventures, management buyouts and buy-ins, academic spin-offs, and social enterprises.

Theme 6 relates to the *outcomes of entrepreneurial endeavours*. The economic and non-economic outcomes of entrepreneurial endeavours relate to the entrepreneur and the firm.

Benefits of entrepreneurial firms

Table 2 illustrates that besides generating personal wealth, entrepreneurs can generate wider benefits. Entrepreneurial firms play a role in the process of economic development. They have a role in reducing unemployment and poverty, including being major creators of new jobs when large firms are downsizing.

Entrepreneurial firms generate individual and employee wealth, which can generate tax revenues. They are also the seeds from which large successful organizations grow (e.g. Microsoft, Cisco Systems, The Body Shop).

Entrepreneurial firms can be flexible and adaptable, enabling them to seize new opportunities. They can stimulate competition, promoting lower prices, more consumer choice, encouraging the creation and dissemination of new innovative products/services and/or better-quality products and services. This competition encourages more efficient use of resources and the displacement of non-viable inefficient businesses. Viable businesses that are more efficient users of resources will be associated with superior levels of productivity, which can enable them to sustain competitive advantage in local and international markets. Efficient entrepreneurial firms that can internationalize can create jobs and wealth, and play a role in reducing balance of payments deficits (or increasing surpluses), thus ensuring a healthy balance between a country's imports and exports. 'Born-global' innovative firms play a role in reducing balance of payments deficits right from their creation.

Few firms are engaged in truly innovative activities. Most new and small firms are imitative, or firms introduce incremental innovations to sustain their competitive advantage. A very small subset of entrepreneurs with unique scientific or technological knowledge creates radical innovations leading to the creation of new industries that promote economic development associated with the destruction of some old industries.

Most entrepreneurial firms are engaged in servicing private consumers (e.g. restaurants and retail outlets) or other enterprises. The servicing relationship between an entrepreneurial firm and its customers can range from cooperation to dependency and exploitation. Many large firms would not be able to remain profitable without the service provided by new and small firms in their supply chain.

Table 2. Entrepreneurial firms: positive economic and non-economic contributions and barriers to enterprise

Positive contributions	Barriers
Economic	*Macro-economic*
Economic development	Taxation, interest and exchange rates public spending, inflation policy, and regulatory framework
Reduce unemployment and poverty	
Job generation when large firms are downsizing	
Wealth creation and taxes to support government policies	
'Seed' firms grow into large 'oak' firms	*Cultural barriers and narrow education base*
Competition, innovation, productivity, and supply-chain benefits	
Internationalization and balance of payments benefit	
Provision of essential services to enhance quality of life	*Advantages of large firms*
Harmonious working environment	
Seedbed nurturing future entrepreneurs	*Attitudinal barriers*
Protect and promote local communities and their development Clusters of knowledge and technology-based firms create spillover, multiplier, job, wealth, and competitiveness benefits	Reluctant to pursue a career in enterprise, and to focus upon firm growth and use external finance and expertise
Votes for policymakers supporting enterprise	
	Resource barriers
Non-economic	Information, finance, premises, skilled labour, machinery, equipment, etc.
Reduce social and regional inequality	
Promote diversity and encourage under-represented groups such as women to become entrepreneurs	

	Operational barriers
Promote choice, self-help, and personal empowerment	Imagination, creativity, innovation, and use of appropriate management and production systems
	Strategic barriers
	Inability to introduce appropriate differentiation
	Government failure
	Government supports wrong firms and entrepreneurs that do not require help

Entrepreneurial firms, especially small firms, can provide a harmonious working environment. This is reflected in fewer industrial disputes and lower absenteeism. They may provide a nurturing role model and learning environment for potential entrepreneurs.

Entrepreneurial firms promote local development and the regeneration of deprived rural and urban communities as they frequently service local markets. The entrepreneur(s) may live close by and feel an allegiance to the area where the firm is located. They generally employ people and suppliers within easy reach. New firm formation (NFF) and growth can generate local multiplier effects that increase the demand for other new firms, which can promote a spiral of wealth creation and job generation to reduce local unemployment and poverty.

Entrepreneurial firms can generate several social benefits. A growing stock of entrepreneurial firms may reduce a dependency culture on the state and larger firms, as well as reduce the power of large firms and trade unions. Entrepreneurial firms provide working and learning contexts that promote choice, opportunity, empowerment, individualism, and self-reliance, particularly for economically disadvantaged groups in society such as women, young people, and ethnic minorities. Promoting entrepreneurship is part of a formula seeking to reconcile economic success with social cohesion.

Barriers

There are different types of entrepreneurial firms and entrepreneurs, with most new firms not desiring or reporting significant employment growth. Only 4 per cent of firms generate 50 per cent of job generation by the firms over a decade. The majority of new firms are born to die young as most cease to trade within three years of inception. Most firms that survive are born small and stay small. Many small firms are more interested in maintaining their current level of profit than in expansion. One reason for firms wishing to stay small is that the ownership and management reside in the same person or persons; so future firm goals are determined not only by commercial considerations but by personal lifestyles and family factors relating to the individuals or teams of individuals who own and manage them. Firm development can be restricted by entrepreneurs who want to maintain ownership and control of their firms, and who may only grow their ventures to an internal management comfort zone, which allows owners to maintain control and ownership. But it seems that the proportion of small businesses that want to grow is greater than the numbers that actually grow.

Table 2 summarizes several broad types of barrier. People need to believe they can be entrepreneurs and have the intention to grow. Government can play a role in addressing attitudinal barriers to enterprise. People need to raise their expectations, individualism, and self-reliance, and they need to believe they can be successful entrepreneurs. In addition, some people face resource, operational, and strategic barriers to NFF and development. People generally report market resource barriers (i.e. access to information, finance, premises, training, skills, compliance costs associated with statutory and regulatory administration, etc.).

Entrepreneurial firms generally have a limited track record. They can be deficient in the amount and type of resources they can mobilize. With inadequate credibility and links with partners they may not have the necessary experience to utilize their limited pool of resources efficiently. New firms can lack the skills both to adapt their product offering to what the market is really looking for, and to be able to gain legitimacy from external stakeholders and resource providers.

These problems comprise the liability of newness and are fourfold. First, new firms need to find resources and time to create new organizational roles and functions, knowledge, and learning. Second, the process of inventing and learning new roles is costly because it requires negotiation with others in the organization to agree new roles, responsibilities, and relationships. Third, reliance on relationships with strangers results in low interpersonal trust and potentially precarious relationships between co-workers. Fourth, new organizations face difficulties in establishing external relationships with other organizations because they have not built stable ties over time, for example with customers and suppliers. In addition, new firms engaged in creating and exploiting new knowledge face the liability of innovation.

Entrepreneurs can adopt behaviour and strategies to mitigate the effects of these liabilities. For example, innovative new firms can establish alliances with incumbent large firms. These links enable them to access resources to develop the technology further, as well as to gain downstream access to final customers when they do not have the sales and marketing skills to do so. Such alliances may be a precursor to the entrepreneur being able to sell the business to reap a capital gain. On the downside, the more powerful larger partner can dictate terms and expropriate some of the entrepreneur's potential gains.

Newness can, however, generate assets. It can bring advantages of flexibility and adaptability to changing market conditions. The phenomenon of internationalizing new ventures, or 'born globals' as noted earlier, shows how some innovative new high-tech firms can take advantage of opportunities in international markets from the beginning.

Policy initiatives

Governments concerned with generating the economic benefits highlighted in Table 2 particularly want to increase the number of technology- and knowledge-based high-growth ventures. Those concerned with reducing social and regional inequality in their countries can also promote people from disadvantaged groups and/or under-represented groups in enterprise to become entrepreneurs (i.e. women, young people, ethnic minorities, etc.). Policy intervention is designed to reduce the barriers faced by such people seeking to establish and grow entrepreneurial ventures.

An array of hard assistance such as grants, equipment, premises, and/or soft assistance such as education, training, information, counselling, mentoring can be provided. Types of intervention to support NFF and development are summarized in Table 3.

Paul Reynolds and colleagues suggest that governments can stifle the efforts of those attempting to start new firms through onerous bureaucratic requirements, complex regulations, or merely through slow reactions to requests for decisions required to form a new firm. There are wide and surprising discrepancies between countries in the hurdles that entrepreneurs need to negotiate to start a new firm. The International Finance Corporation, part of the World Bank, ranks the top three in the world in terms of the ease of starting a new business as New Zealand, Australia, and Canada. The United States arrives in 13th place, behind Saudi Arabia in 10th but ahead of the UK in 19th, France in 25th,

Entrepreneurship

Table 3. Types of government support for new firm formation and development

---

- *Macro policies*
- Interest rates
- Taxation
- Public spending
- Inflation

- *Deregulation and simplification*
- Cutting red tape
- Legislative exemptions
- Legal form

- *Sectoral and problem-specific policies*
- High-tech firms
- Rural enterprises
- Community enterprises/social enterprises
- Cooperatives
- Ethnic business

- *Financial assistance*
- Business Expansion Scheme/Enterprise Investment Scheme
- Loan Guarantee Scheme
- Enterprise Allowance Scheme/Business Start-up Scheme
- Grants

- *Indirect assistance*
- Information and advice
- Business growth training/other formal training
- Accelerator programmes
- Consultancy initiative

- *Relationships*
- Small firm division in the enterprise department
- Lobbyist/policy formulation

Source: Adapted from Storey (1994: 269)

Germany in 98th, Spain in 133rd, Greece in 135th, and China in 151st (http://www.doingbusiness.org/rankings).

Intervention aimed at promoting entrepreneurship to address economic and social issues in regions can be problematical. Nationally applied policies to increase capacity for NFF in all regions can indirectly favour more prosperous and socially and economically well-endowed regions. A non-selective policy of encouraging NFF and growth, with no regional targeting built into it, may enhance regional differences by having relatively modest impacts in regions with existing resource shortages.

General measures to proactively provide a supportive environment for all forms of enterprise may not be cost effective. To promote NFF and development, particularly in hostile environments, governments can directly (or indirectly) support local-level initiatives that reduce uncertainty for entrepreneurs, and/or provide resources to enable more people to circumvent attitudinal, resource, operational, and strategic barriers to NFF and development.

Of course, there is no guarantee that intervention will succeed in promoting entrepreneurial activity that leads to improved economic performance. Intervention can be perceived as correct at the time of introduction, but in the future may generate some undesirable outcomes. Such intervention may have other objectives—notably, increasing votes and the chances of re-election for the government or its party in a locality.

Intervention is associated with costs. David Storey has warned that enterprise intervention policies can only be justified in a market economy where it can be demonstrated that the effect of government intervention will lead to an overall net improvement in welfare to the economy as a whole. If enterprise policy intervention leads to an increase in the number of new smaller firms but also to a compensating, or more than compensating, reduction in

18

employment in large firms, then it is difficult to justify such policies on welfare grounds. Governments therefore need to consider the costs and benefits of the intervention to the recipient as well as to wider society. In other words, intervention needs to involve initiatives that encourage actions that would not otherwise have been undertaken (i.e. input additionality), contributing to better results than would otherwise have been achieved (i.e. output additionality), or changing behaviour in a desired direction (i.e. behavioural additionality). Government may not solely drive policy intervention. Charities and social enterprises discussed in Chapter 6 can fill some gaps. For example, the Prince's Trust Enterprise Programme in the UK supports unemployed young people between 18 and 30 years of age. It promotes business idea generation. It also provides business skills training, legal help, and business planning support to ensure ideas are viable.

There is a tension over whether policy support should focus on stimulating large numbers of new firms or supporting fewer, better-quality firms. Enterprise support focusing on increasing the quantity of new firms irrespective of the entrepreneurs' need, ability, or growth ambitions may generate limited economic benefits. It may be preferable to target support to a smaller number of 'winning' firms, that is, firms with significant wealth creation potential. For example, policies can be targeted at stimulating sectors with the capacity to be world leaders to fulfil their potential. Governments concerned with reducing social and regional inequality recognize the need to target assistance for special groups of entrepreneurs, such as women and people from ethnic minorities.

Support is primarily provided to the individual entrepreneur during the NFF process. After the firm-initiation hurdles have been addressed and the firm has commenced trading, external support for enterprise becomes more focused on the needs of different types of firms (i.e. family, high-technology, exporting firms, etc.). There may be a need to focus upon the entrepreneur, rather than the firm alone, throughout all stages of the entrepreneurial process.

As we shall see in Chapter 4, entrepreneurs are not homogeneous in their human capital profiles, motivations, resources, behaviour, prior entrepreneurial experience, and performance. Different types of entrepreneur may require customized assistance. Recognition of this entrepreneurial diversity contributes toward the development of policies tailored to different types of entrepreneur, rather than the provision of broad blanket policies to all types of entrepreneur, irrespective of need or ability. This means a shift from support aimed at increasing new firm start-ups, only to see large numbers of them fail shortly afterwards, to include customized support that reflects the track record from prior business ownership experience. Support could be allocated to growth-orientated entrepreneurs to ensure that the full economic and societal potential of all businesses they own is realized.

Chapter 2
Discovering and creating opportunities

James Dyson created a new type of bagless vacuum cleaner after recognizing that the suction in his traditional vacuum cleaner became inefficient when its cloth bag filled with particles. There was already a long-established vacuum cleaner market but the new patented technology developed by Dyson fundamentally changed how the demand for labour-saving household cleaning devices was met. Through the long and costly process of developing his new technology, which included borrowing £600,000 to set up his company and developing some 5,000 prototypes, Dyson had to make the judgement that his idea would eventually work and that there would be a market for it.

In the 19th century, Clarence Birdseye discovered the basis for an entirely new type of operation for producing frozen food. Initial efforts to freeze meat and vegetables commercially were unsuccessful because the process took many hours, and the food lost its texture and flavour. He observed that the Inuit Indians' practice of quick-freezing fish retained the flavour when the fish were subsequently cooked. Birdseye developed the technology to reproduce this process commercially. Initially, his business was a financial failure due to scepticism on the part of consumers. Birdseye continued perfecting his idea by developing a new process of packaging food in cartons, and quick-freezing the contents under pressure. The frozen-food industry was born. He sold his company to acquire resources to launch a successful campaign to convince customers of the benefits of the concept. The company then became a commercial success.

Mark Zuckerberg founded the social networking site Facebook. Zuckerberg had developed a reputation as a computer programming prodigy. Prior to developing the idea for Facebook, he had used this skill to develop other sites for fun that included an online directory containing details of students in his university dormitory. By 2010, Facebook had an estimated 500 million users worldwide and had achieved a stock market listing.

All three people would doubtless be regarded as entrepreneurs. But their paths to entrepreneurship differ. These examples illustrate similarities in the general functions of entrepreneurs, and differences in the development of their entrepreneurial opportunities.

Functions of entrepreneurs

The Chicago tradition is associated with Frank Knight who suggests entrepreneurs can be recipients of pure profit, which is their reward for bearing the costs of uncertainty. Knight views uncertainty bearing as the true function of entrepreneurs. Uncertainty relates to a distribution when the outcome is not known. Knight suggests entrepreneurs take risks in an uncertain world. Risk relates to the distribution of the outcomes in a group of instances that is known either through calculation based on theoretical deduction or from statistics of past experience.

For Knight, the function of an entrepreneur is to be a calculated risk taker. Knight recognized that entrepreneurs require foresight and command over resources if they are to back their judgements.

He suggests entrepreneurs have a low aversion to risk because they self-finance their own judgements.

Len Shackle used the term 'enterpriser' rather than entrepreneur. Enterprisers exhibit creativity and spontaneity to address uncertainty. The enterpriser deals with uncertainty, makes skilled judgements, assembles and allocates scarce resources, and provides novel products. Entrepreneurial knowledge, thought, feeling, imagination, and creativity are fused into action to address the absence of complete knowledge resulting from uncertainty.

Mai-Li Hammargren, a student at the Stockholm School of Economics, had a boyfriend whose working hours were different from hers. She reflected on a way to set her alarm clock whilst not waking him up. Her imaginative and creative idea was a vibrating watch with a touch screen that makes it easy to navigate between the timing, timer, and alarm. Her idea won a business idea competition. At the age of 21, while still studying, she and engineering student Oscar Ritzén Praglowski established the Mutewatch company in 2008. The product is now exported throughout the world.

The German–Austrian tradition associated with the work of Joseph Schumpeter addresses the link between instability and economic development. Schumpeter suggests that the entrepreneur is not a risk bearer. Rather, risk bearing is the function of capitalists who provide finance to entrepreneurs. Entrepreneurs bear risk only if they act as capitalists. He asserts that entrepreneurs are the creators and catalysts of dynamic change. Entrepreneurs are special people because they are visionaries. Anyone who fulfils the function of an innovator or conducts new combinations is an entrepreneur. The precursors of innovation are imagination and creativity.

Radical innovation (or novelty) is seen as a prerequisite for genuine entrepreneurship. Schumpeterian innovations are discrete and substantial. Discrete innovations are linked to five sources of significant change or new combinations. First is the introduction of a new good, or an improvement in the quality of an existing good. Second is the opening of a new market, in particular an export market in a new territory. Third is the conquest of a new source of supply of raw materials or half-manufactured goods. Fourth is the introduction of new methods of production as yet unproven. Fifth is the creation of a new type of industrial organization, particularly the formation of a trust or some other type of monopoly.

Radical innovation leads to new products that generate wealth creation and job generation benefits. These new products threaten the continued viability of many existing products/processes. New firms engaged in radical innovation can destroy the traditional markets serviced by existing less-innovative firms. The success of the new venture introducing radical innovation can encourage imitators. Increased uncertainty and competition may lead to the closure of some established and new entrants. Firm closure will continue until the level of profitability in the new industry or process is comparable to the rates of return in established activities. Only the fittest firms in the industry using the appropriate technology and best business practice earn profits and survive. This entrepreneurship that destroys as it creates and creates as it destroys has been termed the cycle of creative destruction.

Lesser entrepreneurs can also introduce a range of new activities, complementary to the original innovative venture. Utilizing the radical technology in new markets and adapting this technology, they may generate additional wealth and job creation not originally envisaged by the Schumpeterian-type entrepreneurs that introduced the radical innovation in the first place. Policymakers seeking to promote economic development, therefore, want to increase the supply of radical innovators in order to generate direct and indirect benefits associated with the original radical innovation.

The overriding motive for entrepreneurial activity is the profit that can result from being the first to innovate a particular process or product. Schumpeter sees these profits as being temporary. In the absence of monopoly protection, others will see the profits available in the new innovation and will emulate the original innovation, providing competition and a gradual erosion of the monopoly profits available. Schumpeter later predicted the demise of the function of the entrepreneur. He believed that teams of workers and scientists operating in large organizations would carry out technological advance and change rather than this being done by entrepreneurs. These teams would more likely have the resources and skills to translate the vision (i.e. the new combination) into a feasible plan of action.

The French tradition is exemplified by the work of Richard Cantillon, who is often associated with the term 'entrepreneur' as discussed in Chapter 1. In early 16th-century France, men engaged in leading military expeditions were referred to as entrepreneurs. The French government in the early 18th century applied the term to road, harbour, and fortification contractors.

Cantillon suggests that entrepreneurs react to profit opportunities, bear uncertainty, and continuously serve to bring about a (tentative) balance between supplies and demands in specific markets. The entrepreneur is a pivotal figure who operates within a set of economic markets. Cantillon used the term 'entrepreneur' to refer to individuals who pursue the profits of arbitrage under conditions of uncertainty. This is the process whereby the prices of the same product in different markets are equated in the absence of transport costs. In undertaking arbitrage, the entrepreneur acts as a speculative middleman linking supply with demand. The entrepreneur is a bearer of uncertainty who might or might not own capital. Actions taken by an entrepreneur are associated with a profit (or loss). The entrepreneur's income is the residual received after all contractual payments have been met. Cantillon presents a broad definition that suggests that anyone who runs a business can be regarded as an entrepreneur.

The Classics tradition, exemplified by Jean-Baptiste Say, emphasizes the multiplicity of roles that the entrepreneur must adopt in order to succeed. His law suggests that supply can create its own demand. Entrepreneurs have the ability to assemble and manage resources. Further, they combine and coordinate the factors of production to reduce risk in order to accommodate the unexpected and overcome problems. Entrepreneurs are not concerned simply with the production process or the product market. They are required to accumulate resources (i.e. raw materials, premises, labour, plant, equipment, finance, etc.) and address any regulatory barriers. A high degree of skill and competence is viewed as a prerequisite for successful NFF and development.

Opportunity discovery or opportunity creation?

Perhaps the biggest debate about what entrepreneurs do concerns whether they discover opportunities that already exist or whether they create them. Key dimensions of each perspective are summarized in Table 4.

Some entrepreneurs discover business opportunities by being alert to gaps in the market. Such alertness involves noticing opportunities that have been hitherto overlooked, and to do so without searching for them. The modern Austrian tradition in economics recognizes that there are constant shifts in the demand and supply for products/services. Within this tradition, Israel Kirzner's entrepreneurs are individuals who are most alert to messages from the economy, which signal some failure of coordination, and potential gains from trade. Entrepreneurs are alert to market disequilibrium (i.e. products demanded by consumers are not being supplied at an appropriate price), and they notice how to exploit the gap in the market by arbitrage. By

Table 4. Opportunity discovery versus opportunity creation

	Discovery theory	Creation theory
Nature of opportunities	Opportunities exist independently of the entrepreneur (exogenous; objective)	Opportunities do not exist independently of the entrepreneur (endogenous; socially constructed)
Nature of entrepreneur	Differs in some important ways from non-entrepreneurs, ex ante	May or may not differ from non-entrepreneurs ex ante; differences may emerge ex post dependent
Nature of decision-making context	Risky (can collect information to estimate probability of outcomes)	Uncertain (cannot collect information to estimate probability of outcomes)
Typical questions	Are entrepreneurs that form and exploit opportunities really different from individuals who do not? How do entrepreneurs estimate the riskiness of their decisions?	How does action by entrepreneurs create opportunities? Are there differences between entrepreneurs who form and exploit opportunities and those that do not cause or effect entrepreneurial action? How can entrepreneurs use incremental, iterative, and inductive processes to make decisions?

Source: Alvarez and Barney (2007)

exploiting a gap in the market, an entrepreneur's firm can move an industry towards equilibrium. The entrepreneurial mindset is composed of alertness that facilitates rapid discovery and exploitation of opportunities, even those that are highly uncertain.

At the start of the 20th century, Austin Reed noticed that growing numbers of white-collar workers descending on the City of London wanted to dress as smartly as their masters, at affordable prices. He opened his first men's tailoring store in 1900 in Fenchurch Street, London, having learnt the tricks of the trade from American retailers and manufacturers. In 1925, Austin Reed launched one of the first affordable ready-to-wear suits. He played a key role in crafting British men's formal fashions, particularly for generations of middle managers. Committed to innovation and readiness to respond to new market directions and retailing practices, he opened an impressive flagship store in Regent Street in London dedicated to tailoring, ready-to-wear clothing, and grooming. The Austin Reed Group with its royal warrants from HM Queen Elizabeth II and HRH The Prince of Wales continues to focus on innovation, design, and quality.

Shi Xiaoyang made the leap from nursing in a Beijing hospital to studying abroad, from being a housewife to becoming a billionaire and the boss of a famous furniture company, from owning a small shop to running a large auto theme park. She is the CEO of the Beijing-based Illinois Investment Company Limited, which is a furniture company targeting middle-class, white-collar workers. When Shi moved with her husband to Singapore she was able to appreciate Western values. She noticed the delicate design of furniture and other household appliances from developed countries. Shi then pursued an interior design major at the University of Chicago and closely watched international fashion trends, garnering information and knowledge relating to high-quality materials, brands, and design concepts. Shi spotted the huge potential of the domestic furniture market in China and, with her husband, established a small furniture factory that produced low-cost Western-style furniture, which generated instant customer recognition. Shi began to research trends and spotted a gap in the market for a unique new classic, postmodernism style. She set up a design shop and started to produce Illinois-style furniture for domestic customers and foreign buyers. Shi now owns a 10,000-square-metre furniture outlet that sells her own brands and those of leading designers. She has also established China's first auto theme park located near Beijing International Airport.

Some entrepreneurs discover business opportunities by searching for them. Kirzner, in addition, highlights a developmental approach to opportunity discovery. The prospect of monopoly profits motivates individuals to search for information, which can be used to spot business opportunities. Some entrepreneurs constantly look for market problems and evaluate solutions to these problems.

Some entrepreneurs accumulate experience and knowledge. The possession of additional knowledge provides opportunities for creative discovery. Jim Fiet's study of repeat entrepreneurs with prior business ownership experience shows that prior knowledge can help focus entrepreneurs' efforts. These entrepreneurs subsequently engage in purposeful searches relating to a narrow range of areas where they have specific prior knowledge.

Entrepreneurs can collect and join information together to discover opportunities. An entrepreneur recognizes an (obvious) opportunity for profitable trade, and has the ability based on their knowledge to exploit the opportunity. Further, an entrepreneur is able to identify suppliers and customers and acts as an intermediary taking advantage of opportunities to trade. Discovery and pursuit of an opportunity can also lead to the collection and analysis of additional data and business opportunities. Individuals with the ability to collect and process information may record a spiral of opportunity discovery and exploitation. Kirzner's theory suggests anyone can be an entrepreneur if there are no barriers to perception.

Yu Yu (also known as Peggy Yu) was born in China. She is a wife and mother, and a co-founder with husband Li Guoqing of Dangdang.com, serving as its co-president. The company is China's largest online retailer and the world's largest retailer of Chinese-language books, movies, and music. Yu graduated from Beijing Foreign Studies University, then worked as an interpreter and secretary. She went to the United States to pursue her studies, subsequently gaining an MBA from New York University. Over ten years working in the United States, she accumulated the capital and experience necessary to become an entrepreneur. In the mid 1990s, Yu noticed the success of the online bookstore Amazon.com and realized there was a gap in the market for a similar service in China. But in China few people were Internet users, and there was no database of books in Chinese in print in China. Despite these drawbacks, she perceived a vast lucrative potential market. Yu met Li Guoqing, a book publisher, in China and they married. In collaboration with her partners, Yu begin to build a large database of information on books in print in China. Yu found foreign investment partners and their finance enabled her to found Beijing Science and Culture Book Information Corporation, whose database of books in Chinese provided the information resource required by Yu and her husband to establish an online bookstore. Whilst this information was being collected, there had been a surge in the number of Internet users in China. In 1999, Yu and her husband founded the Chinese online bookstore Dangdang, and the business reported immediate rapid growth. Yu spotted and exploited a further lucrative business opportunity in 2005 when she transformed Dangdang from an online bookstore to a mass merchandiser.

The views of Kirzner are developed within Scott Shane and Sankaran Venkataraman's opportunity-based conceptualization of entrepreneurship. They suggest that entrepreneurship relates to the sources of opportunities; the processes of discovery, evaluation, and exploitation of opportunities; and the set of individuals who discover, evaluate, and exploit them. They differ from other frameworks in their focus on the existence, discovery, and exploitation of opportunities; their examination of the influence of individuals and opportunities, rather than environmental antecedents and consequences; and their consideration of a broader framework than firm creation alone. Actions of people and the insights from individuals to firms and institutions via modes of exploitation are considered.

Causation

Saras Sarasvathy and colleagues make a distinction between causation approaches to opportunity identification (i.e. opportunities are discovered) and effectuation approaches (i.e. opportunities are created). The causation and effectuation views of Sarasvathy and colleagues on the source of opportunity are summarized in Table 5.

Building upon insights from supply and demand theory of classical economics, the causation (or the select and search) approach highlighted by Kirzner relates to the focus of achieving a desired goal through a specific set of given means. Causation relates to individual decision-making heuristics rooted in prediction. (Heuristics are problem-solving rules of thumb; see Chapter 5). People may discover new opportunities by first looking at the traditional growth areas of a market and the largest unserved segments of the population in that market. This information aids the discovery of the most promising opportunity, which is the one expected to yield the highest returns after adjusting for potential risks. Once the opportunity is selected, individuals can collect additional information, seek external professional advice, and formulate business plans drawing upon market research, feasibility analysis, and competitive analysis to test whether the identified opportunity is profitable. Resources

Table 5. Causation and effectuation views on the source of opportunity

The difference between	The market	The logic	The process
Causation (search and select)	A conscious intent to capture a new, underserved, or latent market. Visionary individuals searching for and exploiting market opportunities.	Person has a finite set of possibilities that can be considered. Does not say how much search is conducted, only that it leads to a given set of possibilities.	Because the goal is predetermined at the start of the venture, it is a static process that does not evolve over the course of the venture. Surprises are seen as bad.
Effectuation (creation and transformation)	Transformation leads to the creation of a new market need that may not be intentional or even the result of foresight or imagination of possible new markets. Possibly, one way to fulfil a person's motivations and/or an unanticipated consequence of people doing things that are possible and worth doing.	Begins with very local possibilities but does not select them. Action to transform possibilities into opportunities.	Dynamic and interactive process. Actions and interactions with committed stakeholders who self-select into the entrepreneurial process that leads to transformations, which may lead to new markets. Surprises are good.

Source: Adapted from Read et al. (2011: 6)

are then accumulated and mobilized to establish a business to exploit the opportunity. The entrepreneur adapts the venture to changing market, technological, and regulatory conditions over time to ensure the venture has a sustained competitive advantage. The causation approach is useful in explaining the success of new firms in predictable environments. It assumes that a new firm is sufficiently similar to an existing business so that historical information will inform the decisions of the new firm, and the external environment is sufficiently stable so that outcomes from the past will be relevant to the current situation and the future.

Mary Fairburn illustrates opportunity-discovery behaviour. She is a portfolio entrepreneur owning several businesses in Scotland. Mary consciously looked to expand into a related business area. Following a deliberate decision to move into the funeral director business, she invested considerable effort into looking at how funerals were managed in the UK and Europe, as well as attending an exhibition on funeral directing in Paris. However, the next business was discovered by 'accident'.

Effectuation

The effectuation approach assumes opportunities are created. Building upon insights from Knight that uncertainty bearing is a function of an entrepreneur, and Schumpeter's new combinations perspective relating to new ways of doing things through transformations, effectuation focuses on using a set of evolving means to achieve new and different goals. Effectuators seek to control and shape the future rather than attempt to predict it. This approach is effective under situations of uncertainty, where entrepreneurs have to deal with a future that is unknown and unknowable. Effectual logic is a type of human heuristics used by expert entrepreneurs in NFF. The future is assumed to be fundamentally unpredictable but can be controlled by human action. Using effectual reasoning, people start with a set of means. During the process of using these means, new and different goals gradually emerge. Effectuation can evoke creative and transformative tactics such as: adding to or subtracting from something existing; reorganizing material that is already there or decomposing and recomposing it; transforming existing artefacts by converting them into new uses; increasing or decreasing or reordering the relative emphasis of features of a product or market; inventing, mirroring, twisting, turning an idea or artefact inside out; deliberately deforming the original idea or concept to create something new; changing the scope of the market by proposing smaller or larger markets; and drawing upon prior experience and memory by associating the current venture with some previous problem or opportunity.

At the start of the opportunity-creation process, entrepreneurs are assumed to have incomplete information. Markets cannot be defined, and consumers are not aware of their future preferences. However, new technologies can emerge, regulatory conditions may change, and available data can be confusing and conflicting.

The five principles of effectuation are as follows. First is the *'bird-in-the-hand'* principle. Effectuators are assumed to use existing means and ask questions relating to: 'who am I?' 'what do I know?' and 'whom do I know?' They then decide what it is possible to do with the existing range of competencies, resources, and networks available, and what new firms and markets can be created with the available resources and competencies (i.e. 'what can I do?'). Effectuators do not wait for the perfect opportunity. It is assumed that they create and transform existing resources in order to generate new opportunities from mere possibilities. Action is based on what is readily available, and they set limits on the amount of resources that can be used to make an opportunity. It is also assumed that the creation of a new market might be the result of an accident or serendipity. Effectuators produce a new market even when they did not intend to as an initial goal. Venture goals emerge during the transformation process.

Second is the '*affordable loss*' principle. Effectuators are assumed to focus on what they can afford to lose, rather than try to predict an ideal return from each opportunity. Third, effectuators are assumed to follow the '*crazy quilt*' principle. They form partnerships with stakeholders willing to make a real commitment to jointly create the future relating to effectuator, product, firm, and market. Effectuators view customers as partners, and quickly sell directly to them in order to learn. Effectuators prefer to create the initial target market segment prior to analysing the competitors. They develop, shape, and define the market themselves rather than find a market. Fourth is the '*lemonade*' principle. Effectuators convert contingencies into resources, embrace surprises that arise from uncertain situations, and remain flexible rather than fixated on existing goals. They focus on unanticipated ends rather than preselected goals, which enables them to turn the unexpected into valuable opportunities, or to turn lemons into lemonade. Fifth is the '*pilot in the plane*' principle. Effectuators do not waste time predicting because they co-create rather than forecast the future.

Bricolage

Entrepreneurs may engage in entrepreneurial bricolage if they are located in a resource-sparse external environment. Bricolage is about making do by applying combinations of the resources at hand to new problems and opportunities. Some entrepreneurs refuse to be constrained by limitations; they improvise, combine existing resources for new purposes, and collect together 'bits and pieces'. Entrepreneurs can recombine elements at hand such as physical resources, labour, skills, competencies, customers, markets, and the institutional and regulatory environment for new purposes.

Three attributes can shape the interaction between entrepreneurs and the market environment. First, entrepreneurs are idiosyncratic in what they perceive to be value-creating resources.

Second, entrepreneurs gain differential benefits from their resource pools based on their creative judgements and actions. Third, even in resource-constrained environments some entrepreneurs perceive resource availability. Because of the nature of the first two attributes, some entrepreneurs can capitalize on resources that other entrepreneurs deem to have less value-creating potential.

Bricolage considers how entrepreneurs in resource-constrained environments make or find opportunities by exploiting institutional, social, and physical resource inputs, which are rejected or ignored by other entrepreneurs. Bricolage can be applied to all four effectuation process steps (i.e. parallel bricolage), or it can be used during one effectuation process step (i.e. selective bricolage). Table 6 summarizes the links between

Table 6. Links between effectuation process steps and bricolage actions

Effectuation	Bricolage
Means-driven transformation: what am I? what do I know? and whom do I know?	What do I have (i.e. resources in hand relating to physical resources, labour, skills, etc.)?
What can I do?/affordable loss	Making do/refusal to be constrained by limitations/creating combinations of resources for new purposes, and collecting together 'bits and pieces'
Interaction with stakeholders	Interaction with customers (i.e. making and becoming friends with customers) and representatives in the institutional environment
Leveraging contingency: new goals and new means	Improvisation/refusal to be constrained by limitations

Source: Solesvik and Westhead (2012)

stages of the effectuation process and bricolage actions. During effectuation process step 1, bricolage is applied when effectuators seek to answer the question 'what do I have?' During step 2, effectuators decide 'what can I do?' and the 'affordable loss' with the current pool of resources, knowledge, and skills. People living where there are formal institutional voids may break the law and use informal institutions, and pay bribes to obtain resources. During step 3, effectuators can accumulate resources by developing strategic alliances and links with competitors. Further, they can accumulate resources by contacting friends to become customers, and ensuring customers become friends. During step 4, effectuators can set new goals, find new means, and can use contingencies to ensure opportunity exploitation. Bricolage actions of recombining resources for new purposes and refusing to be constrained by limitations can be applied.

Adaptation can ensure that appropriate resource combinations are applied to favourable or unfavourable contexts. The current set of resources, competencies, and networks appropriate in one locational and time context may not be appropriate in another context. Effectuators need to constantly adapt and stretch to acquire new competencies, obtain new resources, and/or reconfigure existing resources, and establish new contacts and/or loosen old connections. Effectuators may thus need to constantly repeat steps 1 to 4 to ensure an expanding cycle of resources for opportunity making. To ensure opportunity exploitation, entrepreneurs over time may switch from the effectuation to the causation approach (and vice versa).

Chapter 3
Exploiting opportunities

A key function of the entrepreneur, as we saw in Chapter 1, is to assemble and manage the resources required to discover, create, and exploit an opportunity. Entrepreneurs face major challenges in assembling and configuring the resources they need to exploit opportunities to become revenue-generating products or services. These resources include entrepreneurial resources relating to human capital skills, capabilities, and knowledge, as well as resources with regard to technology, finance, reputation, networks of contacts, and social capital. The challenges arise partly because entrepreneurs generally initially possess very few resources. It is also challenging to persuade outsiders such as funders to contribute resources when an opportunity involves a product or service that may be little more than an idea to serve a market that does not yet exist. Further, it may be extremely difficult to establish with any degree of certainty how big the market will be, and the time it will take to develop the product or service to serve that market. In the information technology sector, product development can be very rapid. In contrast, the development of products in biomedical and health sectors can take many years. This is because it is necessary to continue to develop the science, undertake clinical trials, and surmount various regulatory hurdles. Even after the development of all these resources, longer-term success may still be elusive.

For example, Professor Mark Ferguson developed a technology with the potential to provide an effective treatment that would reduce the burden on the health-care system relating to anti-scarring wound healing. Initial results were sufficiently promising, and Renovo, the company he founded, was able to attract a venture capital (VC) firm to provide £8 million in 2000 to fund the next stage of recruiting business development and clinical trials directors, and to begin clinical trials. Two years later, a further £23 million was raised to fund more trials and recruitment of a director with the skills to develop the business commercially. In 2006, Renovo listed on the stock market in order to raise significant additional finance for development. It was believed that there was a potential £6 billion worldwide market and initial results of trials were positive, almost doubling the share price in the first year, as illustrated in Figure 2. From 2008 Renovo rode a roller coaster of delays, trial failures, and encouraging results from follow-on products and potential licensing agreements. But after recovering to be the sixth highest rising share on the London Stock Market in 2010, in early 2011 the company's flagship product, Juvista, failed to meet its Phase III endpoints and in early 2012 Ferguson, by now non-executive chairman, resigned.

Resources and capabilities

We have already introduced the notion of resources. Resources are stocks of assets either owned or controlled by the entrepreneur. They are attributes of tangible and intangible assets (or capitals) that enable the entrepreneur to develop strategies to achieve a competitive advantage. To be valuable, resources need to possess idiosyncratic, ambiguous, and non-inimitable characteristics.

Financial capital concerns both the amount of funds and the specialist skills that finance providers bring to help develop the

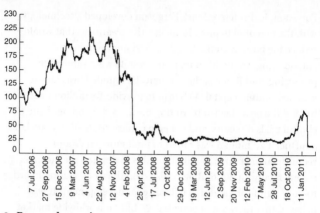

2. **Renovo share price**

venture. Finance can be crucial for acquiring or creating other resources necessary to exploit opportunities, such as the recruitment of specialist personnel and conducting clinical trials, as in the case of Renovo. Firms with strong financial resources have slack, which can facilitate the development of innovations.

Technological capital resources include patents, licences, and other specialist intellectual property (IP). While some technology can be encoded in patents, other technology may be tacit and linked closely to the expertise of the particular entrepreneur. Platform or broad-scope technologies, for example, based on a family of patents, may allow entrepreneurs to develop a range of potential products. This can make the venture more valuable in terms both of future revenue generation and with respect to being attractive to a large firm in the industry that sees possibilities for synergies.

Physical capital relates to the tangible resources of specialist plant and equipment.

Human capital is the set of idiosyncratic skills, capabilities, experience, and knowledge related to a task, and the ability to increase this capital through learning by entrepreneurs. Individuals' motivations, abilities, skills, knowledge, and learning shape their ability to exploit an opportunity and achieve advantage for their firms. Psychological capital relates to the resources possessed by entrepreneurs relating to confidence (or self-efficacy), goal-oriented energy and planning to meet goals, optimism, and resilience (i.e. ability to bounce back). An individual's cognition and knowledge structure can also shape the process of opportunity associated with varying degrees of risk involved. Human capital resources linked to entrepreneurial behaviour are discussed in Chapter 4.

Social capital relates to resources of trust, relationships, and contact networks. A firm's social capital is the sum of its internal social capital (i.e. relationships between individuals) and its external social capital (i.e. relationships between external organizations and individuals in the focal firm). An entrepreneur's social capital can facilitate access to additional resources and knowledge. This social capital can be used to build and mobilize capabilities to create and/or discover opportunities, as well as foster sustained firm competitive advantage. In larger organizations, entrepreneurial individuals with well-developed social skills who create or discover opportunities can gain acceptance for projects that require cross-divisional resources through social networks.

The external environment shapes the ability of entrepreneurs to discover or create opportunities, and their subsequent ability to exploit these opportunities for competitive success. Further, the external environment (or locality) can contain a pool of scarce and valued resources. The level of resource abundance in a particular environment that can support sustained firm survival, stability, and/or growth is termed munificence. The munificence of an environment is context specific for the firm. Entrepreneurs (and

their firms) enter into transactional relationships with the
external environment because they cannot generate all necessary
resources internally.

In dynamic environments, some entrepreneurs and firms develop
and mobilize relationships, networks, and social capital to gain
access to needed resources from partners. They then bundle or
combine these resources together to exploit opportunities.
Cooperative strategies such as alliances can be established to build
capabilities and competitive advantage. Large and small firms
may share ideas, knowledge, expertise, and opportunities to
facilitate collaborative innovation.

A potential downside is that some new entrepreneurial firms can
face difficulties securing resources because they lack legitimacy or
credibility. Notably, some potential suppliers or investors may not
be convinced that the opportunity is viable, and/or may be
concerned that the entrepreneur does not have the ability to
exploit the opportunity, which can generate reluctance for external
investors to become involved.

Resource assembly

At the turn of the 20th century, Alfred Marshall suggested that
the managerial function is both an essential feature of
entrepreneurial activity and a resource. Coordination by an
entrepreneur within an entrepreneurial business leads to novelty
and discontinuity. This insight is important since in themselves
resources do not lead to the exploitation of an opportunity.
Rather, entrepreneurs should have the ability to accumulate,
combine, and mobilize the particular resources required to
exploit the opportunity they have created or discovered. As
entrepreneurial firms evolve, some develop the ability to exploit
and combine resources through organizational routines. Given
the uncertain and often dynamic environment in which they
operate, entrepreneurs need to develop further capabilities that

enable them to reconfigure resources required to adapt to the changed market circumstances.

Entrepreneurs and entrepreneurial firms differ in their ability to handle the variety of resources they need. This resource heterogeneity is a source of difference in their ability to exploit opportunities successfully, and the choice they make regarding which opportunities are exploited.

Some inputs into the entrepreneurial process are interchangeable between any business, while some make a specific contribution to the value of the entrepreneur's venture. Jay Barney's insight is that achieving a sustained competitive advantage for an entrepreneurial venture requires resources that are idiosyncratic to the firm, which are valuable, rare, and neither perfectly imitable (i.e. a valuable resource is controlled by only one firm) nor substitutable without great effort. These resources can be tangible or intangible, and accumulated from the internal and external environment of the venture. Firms differ in the resources they control, and these resources may not be mobile between firms.

Strategic entrepreneurship

Strategic entrepreneurship (SE) focuses attention on understanding how entrepreneurs and entrepreneurial firms create wealth by bringing together unique packages of resources to exploit the opportunities they have created or discovered. SE involves the integration of entrepreneurial and strategic perspectives in developing and taking actions that result in value. An entrepreneurial perspective can be defined as opportunity-seeking behaviour, while a strategic perspective is advantage-seeking behaviour that involves creating and sustaining one or more competitive advantages as the path through which opportunities are exploited. This strategic approach challenges large, established firms to learn to become more entrepreneurial, and challenges smaller entrepreneurial firms to learn how to become more strategic.

The SE approach incorporates environmental, organizational, and individual factors into the process of simultaneous opportunity- and advantage-seeking behaviours. Mike Hitt and colleagues represent SE as a multilevel input–process–output model, as illustrated in Figure 3. First, resources serve as inputs into the SE process at different levels, including environmental factors, organizational factors, and individual resources. Second, SE-related actions or processes focus on the orchestration of resources and the entrepreneurial actions that are used to protect and exploit current resources, while simultaneously exploring for new resources with value-creating potential. Third, the consequent outcomes create value for society, organizations, and individuals. These benefits include societal enhancements, wealth, knowledge, and opportunity.

Firms with an entrepreneurial culture fostering new ideas, creativity, risk taking, and organizational learning can undertake opportunity-seeking behaviour. Effective firm leadership is required to develop and grow new ventures, and to entrepreneurially lead established corporations. Such leadership may influence others to emphasize opportunity-seeking and advantage-seeking behaviours.

To engage in SE, the human, social, financial, and technological resources outlined above are required. Human and social capital are important for achieving and sustaining a competitive advantage, whilst financial capital is often crucial for acquiring or creating the resources necessary to exploit opportunities. An individual's goals, passion, human capital, and mindset can also shape entrepreneurial action through the discovery and creation of new opportunities. As highlighted in Chapter 2, the process of discovering new opportunities can be related to Kirzner's alertness perspective (i.e. opportunities are found).

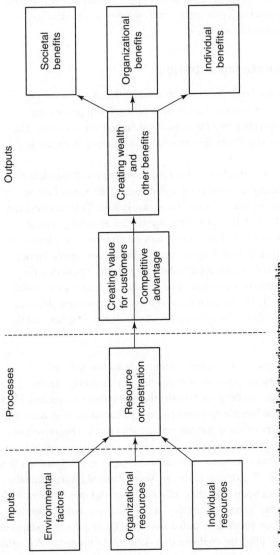

Inputs

Environmental factors

Organizational resources

Individual resources

Processes

Resource orchestration

Creating value for customers

Competitive advantage

Outputs

Creating wealth and other benefits

Societal benefits

Organizational benefits

Individual benefits

3. **Input–process–output model of strategic entrepreneurship**

In addition, the creation of new opportunities can be related to Sarasvathy's effectuation and creativity perspective (i.e. opportunities are made).

Resource orchestration

Entrepreneurs need to control valuable and rare resources. To ensure sustained firm competitive advantage over time, entrepreneurs need to combine or orchestrate resources. The resource orchestration process is summarized in Figure 4.

Actions that structure the firm's resource portfolio relate to acquiring, accumulating, and divesting resources. Further, resources can be bundled into capabilities. This bundling can involve stabilizing existing capabilities, enriching current capabilities, and pioneering new capabilities. The capabilities can then be mobilized to create value for customers. Here a sequence of actions can create, coordinate, and deploy the appropriate set of capabilities needed to ensure a successful strategy. The actual form of resource orchestration depends upon a firm's life-cycle phase, the strategies adopted, and the level of the firm.

With respect to an entrepreneurial firm's life cycle, an opportunity-refinement competency or capability can, for example, be developed during the opportunity-recognition phase. This enables the entrepreneur to mobilize or build on links with industry contacts that have expertise in that particular sector. Competencies in acquiring resources and being committed to a firm, that is having a championing competency, help drive a firm forward. This competence can be constructed through initially building upon links with colleagues. For example, in the case of academic entrepreneurs this can be links with fellow scientists who have previously started a venture. During the early stages of a firm's life cycle, configuration skills will be needed to shape the extent to which the technological resource is a platform

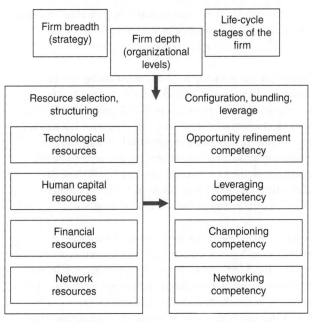

4. Resource orchestration

technology, and to identify the nature of products that can
emanate from it.

Strategies

Entrepreneurial firms can engage in contrasting strategies. At
one end of the spectrum, the strategy can involve the desire to
become a world leader through penetrating international markets
and eventually realizing a stock market listing. At the other end of
the spectrum, a lifestyle business can embark on a strategy to
serve a local market. In the former, entrepreneurial firms may be
able to develop a 'learning advantage of newness' competency.
Their newness can give the firm greater organizational
malleability, enabling the firm to adapt quickly to uncertain

overseas markets. The competence-boosting effects of this early internationalization can then provide these firms with an advantage in developing their domestic markets.

Young entrepreneurial firms that internationalize can be vulnerable if they make significant errors due to a lack of experience. Forming partnerships and alliances with VC firms and customers that have international experience is a way to compensate for this lack of experiential learning. Also, it can enable some young entrepreneurial firms to orchestrate the resources required for successful internationalization. An alternative is to attract team members with international experience to become partners in the founding team.

In larger, established organizations engaged in corporate entrepreneurship (see Chapter 6), the orchestration of resources involves the coordination of the expertise of top, middle, and lower management. For example, lower-level management who are closer to specific customers can be well placed to convey knowledge that helps in the orchestration of resources to best serve the market.

In new entrepreneurial firms, such as academic spin-offs (see Chapter 6), orchestration can involve building deeper commercial and technological human capital resources. Development of these resources needs to be synchronized for the spin-off to be able to identify, shape, and meet a new market need. This synchronization may be achieved by building boards and management teams, as well as through the incubator context where the spin-off is nurtured.

High-tech start-up firms, such as academic spin-offs, often need to develop both an executive board of directors and a scientific advisory board with the specific competences to exploit a particular opportunity. Incumbent executives in the spin-off firm on their own, especially if their background is as academic scientists, may not have the commercial knowledge or abilities to understand a changing competitive landscape and specific challenges of industry and markets. Selecting the right mix of directors with unique and useful skills or connections can improve the spin-off's competitive advantage. Boards in spin-off firms can be more effective when skilled directors with knowledge of how to commercialize early-stage technology have been recruited to help the firm fully realize its potential. A major shortcoming concerns the challenges in overcoming resistance from spin-off founders to outsiders entering the firm with different views about the best way to orchestrate resources.

Successfully exploiting an opportunity invites imitation from competitors. Proactive actions such as copyrights, patent protection, and negotiated contracts can discourage imitation. Patent protection can increase a firm's ability to appropriate rents from innovation. Entrepreneurs can use copyrights and patent protection to protect their ideas and resources or forestall others from appropriating value from them. The protection of intellectual property and complementary resources is critical to the appropriation of value that resource orchestration creates.

Benefits

The processes and actions comprising SE can generate several potential beneficial outcomes. Besides financial wealth, *individual* entrepreneurs can generate socio-emotional wealth (i.e. self-actualization and satisfaction in developing an independent business). Entrepreneurial learning from experience enables entrepreneurs to enhance their cognitive resources (i.e. perceptual acuity, memory). The latter enable entrepreneurs to build their personal knowledge stocks, in turn leading to more accurate recognition, evaluation, and exploitation of additional business opportunities.

There are several benefits for *firms*. For example, firms can break into an established market or create a new market. They may develop a product that is highly differentiated from existing products and one that creates substantial value for customers. Firms may create new technologies or develop radical innovations with value-creating potential that enables them to achieve competitive advantage. After firms capture a market-leading position they often engage in incremental innovation to improve their product in order to stay ahead of competitors. In contrast, firms introducing new technologies and innovation can create new knowledge. This in turn can provide new market opportunities to introduce a new product or create a new market.

There can be benefits for *society*. New firm creation, sustained competitive advantage, and growth can contribute positively to additional economic activity (i.e. job creation, technological advancement, and economic stability and growth), as well as the potential for other social benefits. Further, it can promote a new culture of social entrepreneurship (see Chapter 6) leading to the creation of new non-profit firms that enrich the natural environment and/or are designed to overcome or limit others' negative influences on the physical environment.

Business plan and business model

Entrepreneurs develop business plans that set out the nature of the business, its intended market and customers, and the resources it needs to achieve its goals of meeting a perceived market need. Entrepreneurs can develop both informal and formal business plans. Informal business plans are utilized as an operational guide to facilitate a new firm's development. The formal business plan is a key document for attracting the initial attention of a financier such as a bank, local enterprise development agency, business angel, and/or a formal VC backer. Formal VC firms, for example, generally fund a very small percentage of the large number of business plans they receive each month. Consequently, the business plan must clearly highlight that the entrepreneur seeking finance has a credible investment opportunity, which offers the potential for a significant return on investment. The business plan should cover the following issues: all major activities of the business, financial projections, a detailed and coherent strategy for achieving projected performance, details of the funding which is sought, and the expected timing and nature of returns for the investor. Key elements of a business plan are illustrated in Table 7.

The entrepreneur may need to make use of professional and independent advice to shape the business plan. This external validity can be used to sell the entrepreneur's investment proposition to a VC firm. However, the VC firm will want to see the entrepreneur's (or entrepreneurial ownership team's) ideas and expertise clearly reflected in the business plan, and not those of someone else. The major areas of weakness in business plans of new-technology-based firms (NTBFs) relate to marketing and the management team, followed by financial aspects, primarily because the entrepreneurs involved in such ventures tend to have technological rather than commercial backgrounds.

Although business plans are widely used by entrepreneurs, their usefulness is debatable. One potential problem is that they are static documents, which may have severe shortcomings for early-stage firms, where neither the product nor the market is well defined. The assumptions on which the business plan is based can be seriously misleading when the entrepreneur comes into contact with the reality of the marketplace. More recent practice emphasizes the need for an entrepreneur to develop a business model. This focuses the entrepreneur to consider how the business would create, deliver, and capture value to customers. The business model reflects management's assumptions about what customers want, how they want it, and how a firm can organize to best meet those needs. The value of the business model is to show how the parts of the business are orchestrated together to produce

Table 7. Elements of a business plan

Section	Key features
Executive summary	Short summary of the purpose of the plan and key aspects of the plan, including the funding sought to achieve them (i.e. milestones)
The business	Brief business history, progress, and organization that are relevant to future development
Management and employees	Details of the management team's past experience and future role; gaps in management that need to be filled; employee numbers and skills mix
Products/Services	Description of products or services; distinctive competence of products/services in the market; state of technology involved; range of products/services (current and future)
The market and competition	Size and expected market growth; domestic and international mix; market segments; current and expected customers
Marketing	Current and expected approaches to marketing and pricing
Operations and production strategy	Existing production facilities and future developments; suppliers
Investment proposal	Amount of funding sought; expected ownership stakes, valuations, and returns; timing and nature of realization of future gains for investors

Financial information	Up to three years' historical financial information and up to three years' detailed financial projections, including cash-flow statements; banking arrangements; state of order book; sensitivity analyses and assumptions underlying them; nature of financial control systems
Risks and milestones	Main areas of risk and milestones and how they will be addressed
Appendices	Details of management curricula vitae, patents, etc. as appropriate

the product/service, how supplies will be accessed, how the product/service will be distributed to customers, and how revenues will flow into the business over time. This business-model approach encourages entrepreneurs to interact with the potential market at an early stage. It enables the entrepreneur to develop more realistic insights into the revenue model, pricing, resources, and costs involved in acquiring customers and suppliers. For example, a 'bricks and clicks' business model involves a firm integrating both offline (i.e. bricks) and online (i.e. clicks) presence in the market place. A chain store can, for example, allow the user to order products online but pick up their order at a local store.

Chapter 4
Entrepreneurs' context

Debate surrounds whether entrepreneurs are born or made. Why this should be more of an issue for entrepreneurs than for, say, physicists or accountants is frankly puzzling. Nevertheless, a central question that has preoccupied the entrepreneurship literature is: *Is it an individual's personality or their socialization process that shapes their propensity to become an entrepreneur?* On the one hand, an individual's personality, loosely defined in terms of their regularities in action, feeling, and thoughts, is held to explain their actions. This approach adopts the position that the possession of inborn personality traits predisposes an individual towards enterprising behaviour.

On the other hand, social and career employment history contexts may shape an individual's propensity to become an entrepreneur or successful entrepreneur. Social contexts can shape the supply and demand for entrepreneurial behaviour. Key social context dimensions are social class, family composition, and parental background. Social context can shape an individual's expectations, access to higher-quality education, ability to obtain a job, and ability to obtain an employment position. It can promote the accumulation of financial resources and human capital resources in the form of managerial, technical, and entrepreneurial capabilities. Therefore social context shapes access to resources that can either promote or retard an individual's desire to become an entrepreneur, and their subsequent career in entrepreneurship. This perspective has clear implications for the development of policy to stimulate entrepreneurship. Practitioners may assume that the supply (and quality) of entrepreneurs can be increased if the external environment is manipulated to encourage more people to gain access to information, education, and training that foster entrepreneurial attitudes and resources.

Major differences between the personality 'born' view and social development 'made' view are summarized in Table 8. The personality perspective is summarized in Chapter 5. Here we discuss the links between an individual's social context and the attitudes and resources that can be accumulated at different stages of life, which can be mobilized to pursue a career in enterprise.

Social process

Entrepreneurial ideas and ambitions can evolve in a social context. These contexts can shape the supply and demand for entrepreneurial behaviour. A person's social context shapes their access to resources that can foster or block an entrepreneurial career. Social context can constrain a person's career decisions. The decision to become an entrepreneur may be limited by the expectations and experience individuals face in the social world. Also, individuals can be socialized to behave in ways that meet with the approval of their role set. Dominant values of close associates may translate into expectations that shape individual behaviour.

The social development perspective presented by Allan Gibb and John Ritchie suggests that the types of situations people encounter and the social groups to which they belong throughout their life course shape the attitudes and resources required to engage in the entrepreneurial process. Social factors that shape individuals' entrepreneurial ideas and ambitions at different stages of life are summarized in Table 9. A distinction is made

Table 8. Views on new small business development and the individual

	Personality 'born' view	Social development 'made' view
Formation of basic motivation	Assumed to be inborn and determined relatively early in life	Assumed to be the result of a wide range of influences through life (including class, family, education, career)
Influences during adult life on desire to become an entrepreneur	Desire comes from within; is a response to personality	Is the result of interaction with others
Acquisition of new business ideas	Explained by chance, fortune, and fate as well as the given personality traits	Explained as an ongoing process with a degree of pattern and predictability according to both the knowledge of the individual and the range of social situations the person finds themselves in
Explanation of the business entry decision	Seen as an individual and personal event: the new entrepreneur is 'born', not made, with an almost subconscious search for the 'right' opportunity	Can be explained in terms of group interaction and pattern of life
Associated interventionist philosophy by government	Because entrepreneurship involves 'natural selection', then external intervention seen as essentially marginal; activity is therefore best directed toward removing assumed environmental obstacles such as taxation	Belief that social intervention can activate the individual and environment to desired ends

Table 9. Influences on the development of entrepreneurial ideas and ambitions at different stages of life

Childhood	Adolescence	Early adulthood	Middle adulthood	Late adulthood
Parental and wider family class and class mobility	Parental and wider family influence on vocational preference	Choice of further education/training	Occupational and class mobility	Class attained and income/wealth achieved
Parental and wider family work situation	Choices of vocational education available	Own class ranking	Nature of work	Family situation
Parental and wider family educational choice	Education as provider of values and goals	Friendship and community attachment	Own family and friendship	Communal attachments
Parental and wider family values and life goals	Friendship and community attachments	Residual family influence	Working relationships	Extra work opportunities
		Possible own family	Reward systems and job satisfaction	Job satisfaction
		Nature of work	Interactions with environment socially and at work	Pensions and early retirement facilities
			Business training and development	

Source: Gibb (1987: 13)

57

between stages of childhood, adolescence, early adulthood, middle adulthood, and late adulthood. The nature of early life experience can be especially formative in creating basic ambitions, but adulthood can shape entrepreneurial ideas and ambitions. Several factors illustrated in Table 9 potentially shape the evolution of individual entrepreneurial ambitions, ideas, thinking, skills, and experience.

Socio-economic factors considered relate to social class, family composition, and parental background. These factors may impact opportunity structures and entrepreneurial decision-making. Parental role models can raise expectations and encourage family members to become business owners. For example, children drawn from families associated with business ownership are more likely to pursue careers as business owners. An individual's age, education, and employment history may shape expectations and access to resources, which can be mobilized to create, discover, and exploit opportunities. Age can impact on the decision to own a business: a person under 30 could lack resources, while one over 45 might lack energy.

Length of work experience and relevance of that experience (e.g. industry-specific knowledge) can impact the decision to become an entrepreneur. Entrepreneurial decisions may be shaped by the type and size of incubator organization (i.e. previous employer prior to business ownership), and the extent to which it allowed individuals to develop problem-solving skills. Some locations and social contexts have institutions that seek to address attitudinal, resource, operational, and strategic barriers to NFF and development.

The social development perspective does not tell us exactly what resources, skills, and capabilities are needed to discover, create, and exploit opportunities. This perspective can, however, be used to describe entrepreneurs, and to explore the diverse nature of entrepreneurship.

Human capital

Nobel Prize winner Gary Becker suggests that an individual's human capital profile shapes productivity. An entrepreneur's demographic characteristics, achieved attributes, and accumulated work experience are expected to have a positive (or negative) impact on productivity. We can distinguish between general and specific human capital. General human capital relates to a person's age, gender, ethnic background, social class, education, etc. Specific human capital concerns management and industry know-how, technical and entrepreneurial capabilities, ability to acquire resources, prior business ownership experience, etc. Many human capital variables are shaped by an individual's social context before and during the entrepreneurial process.

Some entrepreneurs can adapt and improve their chances of accessing and mobilizing resources required to circumvent barriers to NFF and development. However, individuals in society differ in their willingness to become entrepreneurs. An individual's resource pool can shape their propensity to pursue a career in entrepreneurship. Studies monitoring regional variations in NFF rates consider the resource profiles of the population living in a locality (i.e. endogenous/supply-side issues) and the external environmental context (i.e. exogenous/demand-side issues) and link these to entrepreneurship.

Pioneering work by Paul Reynolds and colleagues explored the underlying processes associated with the geography of NFF rates in a study of seven developed economies. Each country study focused on two dependent variables relating to firm births in all economic sectors in regions, and manufacturing firm births in regions. Two methods were used to control for the differing sizes of regions. The first was the number of new firms in a region over the study period per 100 firms in that region prior to the study period. This is termed the ecological approach, and analyses the extent to which the business sector is being rejuvenated. The second was the number of new firms in a region over the study period per 10,000 population in that region prior to the study period. This is termed the labour market approach, and explores how entrepreneurial a region's people are.

Considerable variation in NFF rates between European community countries on both these measures was found. Differences in NFF rates were influenced by the relative importance of seven entrepreneurial processes, which are summarized in Table 10. NFF was most strongly encouraged by: growth in demand generated by income and population growth; urbanized/agglomeration context reflecting the advantages of agglomeration (i.e. benefits of access to customers, source of

Table 10. Regional variations in new firm formation rates across seven European Community countries

Entrepreneurial process	All economic sectors	Manufacturing only
Demand growth	Positive (6) [1]	Positive (6)
Urbanization/Agglomeration	Positive (6)	Positive (5)
Unemployment	Positive (4)	Mixed (5)
Personal, household wealth	Positive (3)	None (4)
Small firms/Specialization	Positive (6)	Positive (7)
Political ethos	Positive (2)	Positive (2)
Government spending/Policies	None (4)	Positive (1)
Predictive success		
(Average–median–explained variance)		
Births/10,000 people	78%	60%
Births/100 firms	65%	32%

Note: [1] Indicates the number of countries where one or more indicators of the process could be included

Source: Reynolds et al. (1994: 451)

supply, as well as awareness of competitors' actions); and small firms' skills, expertise, and knowledge context (i.e. incubators where people can develop management and industry know-how, as well as technical and entrepreneurial capabilities).

Building on this work, Paul Reynolds subsequently developed the GEM Index in 1999 to compare entrepreneurship across a greater number of countries worldwide. GEM measures differences in the level of entrepreneurial activity between countries based on two general factors and nine entrepreneurship framework conditions. The two general factors are basic requirement and efficiency enhancers. They are assumed to affect entrepreneurship because without a solid institutional foundation entrepreneurship-specific factors would not be able to function effectively. The nine selected entrepreneurship framework conditions are: the availability of entrepreneurial finance; government policy; government entrepreneurship programmes; entrepreneurship education; R&D transfer; internal market openness; physical infrastructure for entrepreneurship; commercial and legal infrastructure for entrepreneurship; and cultural and social norms. These conditions contribute to the grouping of economies into the following three levels: factor driven, efficiency driven, and innovation driven based on the World Economic Forum's (WEF) Global Competitiveness Report. This report identifies three phases of economic development based on GDP per capita, and the share of exports comprising primary goods. The marked differences in overall entrepreneurship rates between countries highlighted in Figure 5 mask variations in inclusiveness (notably, women and different age groups), the sectors in which businesses are started, and the growth and innovative ambitions of entrepreneurs.

Types of entrepreneur

Social context variables relating to an individual's general and specific capital can be categorized to illustrate distinct entrepreneur

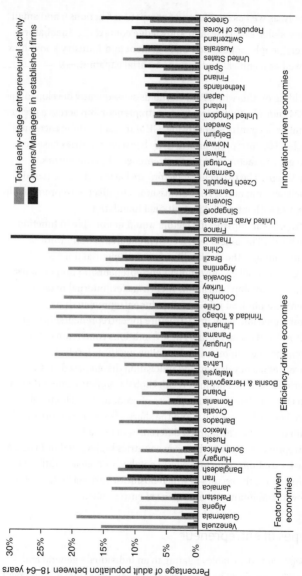

5. Overall entrepreneurship rates between countries 2011

Legend:
- Total early-stage entrepreneurial activity
- Owners/Managers in established firms

Y-axis: Percentage of adult population between 18–64 years (0% to 30%)

Innovation-driven economies:
Greece, Republic of Korea, Switzerland, Australia, United States, Spain, Finland, Netherlands, Japan, Ireland, United Kingdom, Sweden, Belgium, Norway, Taiwan, Portugal, Germany, Czech Republic, Denmark, Slovenia, Singapore, United Arab Emirates, France

Efficiency-driven economies:
Thailand, China, Brazil, Argentina, Slovakia, Turkey, Colombia, Chile, Trinidad & Tobago, Lithuania, Panama, Uruguay, Peru, Latvia, Malaysia, Bosnia & Herzegovina, Poland, Romania, Croatia, Barbados, Mexico, Russia, South Africa, Hungary

Factor-driven economies:
Bangladesh, Iran, Jamaica, Pakistan, Algeria, Guatemala, Venezuela

(and firm) types. These classifications highlight contrasting entrepreneur attitudes, motivations, resource assets and liabilities, behaviour, and/or best (and worst) entrepreneur/firm practice.

Norman Smith presented an insightful typology of types of entrepreneur. Table 11 shows that craftsmen entrepreneurs have a blue-collar background, with limited educational and managerial experience, with a preference for technical work, and they are generally motivated by a need for personal autonomy. Conversely, opportunist entrepreneurs typically have higher levels of education and broader experience, with a motivation to build a successful organization and achieve financial gains. These two types of entrepreneur have contrasting potential for job generation and wealth creation. However, debate continues over the predictive power of the craftsman–opportunist dichotomy. Nevertheless, classifications highlight that entrepreneurs (and entrepreneurial ventures) are not a homogeneous entity.

Ian MacMillan reckons that to really learn about entrepreneurship we need to study habitual entrepreneurs. Here an individual's

Table 11. Smith's profiles of craftsman and opportunist entrepreneurs

Craftsman	Opportunist
• Narrow education	• Broader education
• Blue-collar background	• Middle class
• Successful worker	• Variety of work experience
• Identifies with a task rather than with management	• Identifies with management
• Paternalistic	• Delegates more
• Utilizes personal relationship in marketing	• Market orientated
• Finance from savings and family only	• Many sources of finance
• Rigid strategies followed	• Diverse and innovative competitive strategies

human capital is viewed through a dynamic rather than a static lens. Rather than only being involved in one venture, entrepreneurs can vary in the nature and extent of their prior business ownership experience (PBOE). In our own research, we made a distinction between inexperienced novice entrepreneurs with no PBOE to mobilize, and habitual entrepreneurs with PBOE. Business ownership and a decision-making role within the venture are important dimensions of entrepreneurship. Given the prevalence of team-based entrepreneurship, this ownership may involve minority or majority equity stakes. Adopting a perspective that recognizes that ownership is a key element of entrepreneurship, novice (or one-time) entrepreneurs versus habitual entrepreneurs can be defined. *Novice entrepreneurs* are individuals with no prior minority or majority firm ownership experience, either as a firm founder or as purchaser of an independent firm, who currently own a minority or majority equity stake in an independent firm that is either new or purchased.

Habitual entrepreneurs are individuals who hold or have held a minority or majority ownership stake in two or more firms, at least one of which was established or purchased. Habitual entrepreneurs can be subdivided into serial and portfolio entrepreneurs. *Serial entrepreneurs* are individuals who have sold/closed at least one firm in which they had a minority or majority ownership stake, and currently have a minority or majority ownership stake in a single independent firm. *Portfolio entrepreneurs* are individuals who currently have minority or majority ownership stakes in two or more independent firms.

The emerging opportunity-based conceptualization of entrepreneurship, discussed in Chapter 2, suggests that entrepreneurship involves the discovery, creation, and exploitation of at least one business opportunity. In contrast to views of entrepreneurship that focus on NFF, this approach recognizes that a business opportunity can be exploited through NFF, the purchase of an existing private firm, the discovery and creation of new opportunities in existing firms, or the discovery and creation of opportunities for self-employment. This variety gives rise to a categorization of the nature of habitual entrepreneurship in terms of the modes through which it can occur. A categorization of habitual entrepreneurship is summarized in Table 12. The habitual entrepreneurs covered by cells 1 to 5 engage in entrepreneurship sequentially, while those covered by cells 6 to 10 engage in concurrent entrepreneurial activities. The entrepreneurs in cells 1 and 6 are involved in the founding of new independent firms, while those in cells 2 and 7 are involved in new firms that are spin-offs from other organizations.

The entrepreneurs in cells 3 and 8 have become owners of established independent firms. These acquisitions include individuals from outside the firm who undertake a straight purchase or a management buy-in (MBI) and individuals from inside the firm who undertake a management buyout (MBO) of the firm. Some of these buyouts can involve founders selling their businesses and subsequently buying them back when the acquirers find themselves unable to generate adequate performance because they do not possess the tacit knowledge of the founder. Further, some of these buyouts are secondary buyouts where the same management acquires a larger stake in the firm through a financial restructuring, which may be associated with initial private equity investors selling their shares (we discuss buyouts further in Chapter 6). Entrepreneurs in cells 4 and 9 are engaged as corporate entrepreneurs in existing firms, and they have not purchased the firm. Entrepreneurs in cells 5 and 10 are self- employed individuals who do not form a specific legal entity. We return to these different modes of entrepreneurship in Chapter 6.

Habitual entrepreneurs account for high proportions of owners of private firms in countries such as the UK (52 per cent), United States (51 per cent to 64 per cent), Finland (50 per cent),

Table 12. Categorization of habitual entrepreneurship

Nature of entrepreneurship		Serial entrepreneurs	Portfolio entrepreneurs
Involving new business(es)	De novo business	Serial founders (1)	Portfolio founders (6)
	Spin-off (including corporate & university spin-offs)	Serial spin-out entrepreneurs (2)	Portfolio spin-out entrepreneurs (7)
Involving existing business(es)	Purchase (including buyouts/buy-ins)	Serial acquirers (e.g. secondary MBOs/MBIs) (3)	Portfolio acquirers (e.g. leveraged build-ups) (8)
	Corporate entrepreneurship	Serial corporate entrepreneurs (4)	Portfolio corporate entrepreneurs (9)
Involving no new legal entity	Self-employment	Serial self-employed (5)	Portfolio self-employed (10)

Source: Adapted from Ucbasaran et al. (2008: 111)

Australia (49 per cent), Norway (47 per cent), Sweden (40 per cent), and Malaysia (39 per cent). Experienced entrepreneurs, armed with resources and learning gleaned from PBOE, may more easily overcome obstacles to starting, purchasing, and growing their businesses than do first-time entrepreneurs. As a result of this expected learning, the potential for habitual entrepreneurs to create both greater personal financial returns and greater benefits for society through the development of businesses that create more employment and growth, as well as the generation of higher tax revenue, is of great interest.

Female entrepreneurs

Women are commonly believed to have more communal qualities relating to expressiveness, connectedness, relatedness, kindness, supportiveness, and timidness. Conversely, men are assumed to be associated with more agentic qualities such as independence, aggressiveness, autonomy, instrumentality, and courage. With regard to descriptive stereotypes relating to how men and women are, and prescriptive stereotypes relating to how men and women should be, there are commonly gender-typical roles and consensual beliefs. Men are generally viewed as more agentic and competent than women. From a sociocultural perspective, stereotypes about women and men can relate to gender-typical social role stereotypes. Women can be viewed as homemakers. However, men are widely seen as the breadwinners. These assumed roles heighten consensual beliefs about the attributes of women and men. Culturally produced and socially learned gender stereotypes can manifest themselves in a perceived incongruity between the feminine and the entrepreneur leader role, and the attribution of entrepreneurial abilities. People generally associate masculine characteristics with entrepreneurs. This is termed gender identification. The phenomenon of 'think entrepreneur, think male' tallies with the concern that 'entrepreneurial theories are created by men, for men, and applied to men.' Women can face prejudice. This prejudice can occur in situations that heighten perceptions of incongruity between the feminine gender role and the entrepreneurial leadership role.

Women that perceive a lack of fit between themselves and the masculine stereotype associated with entrepreneurship can negatively evaluate their ability to engage in entrepreneurship. Also, they can perceive a negative evaluation by potential resource providers (i.e. financiers, suppliers, etc.) and by the other men in their lives whose support they need to engage in entrepreneurship. These negative evaluations can deter some women from pursuing careers in entrepreneurship. This can be due to the perception that they will be less rewarded for some behaviour.

Women are largely concentrated in low-status, low-paid work. They often have to surmount attitudinal and resource barriers to business ownership. Hurdles faced by women related to gender and social role are summarized in Table 13. This table also illustrates the motives, resource, and behaviour of women that can shape their propensity to become entrepreneurs, and the success of their firms. Due to these hurdles women are generally under-represented in the entrepreneurial pool.

Women report diverse reasons for pursuing careers in enterprise, including addressing social and labour market discrimination; a route to combat a 'glass ceiling' relating to workplace discrimination that blocks any chances of advancement within an organization; and a coping strategy that provides greater flexibility to accommodate both work and family responsibilities. Entrepreneurship can provide women with freedom to create their own development path based on their own needs, interests, capabilities, and dreams. It can open doors to enable women to fulfil their needs, and employ their feminine intuition, style, skills, experiences, and knowledge. It can also provide women with the independence to decide on and control their own time schedule, tasks, and work pace, and provide greater flexibility in combining work and family responsibilities.

Marie Louise Roy illustrates a journey toward the 'true freedom' that can be achieved through entrepreneurship. Her entrepreneurial journey started with a turbulent childhood in Canada's eastern provinces, through employment exposures in an haute couture workshop, a part-time job in a local department store, a position as a research assistant in a laboratory, as an architect and urban designer with environmental ethics values, and later as artist, writer, author, composer, and singer. She has a diploma from the University of Montreal and a master's degree in applied sciences. Marie Louise is a mother and a determined creative entrepreneur. She runs her own business as a consultant in ecological design and sustainable development (i.e. ecovillages) from the suburbs of Montreal. She pursues her entrepreneurial career by spiritually assisting people, writing books, delivering workshops, and producing CDs.

Over the past decades, there has been a marked increase in the number of women owning businesses. Women are still, however, less likely than men to start and own a business. For example, in the UK 44 per cent of the economically active population are women but only 27 per cent of the self-employed adults are women. Nevertheless, female entrepreneurs on their own or in entrepreneurial teams make notable contributions to wealth creation and job generation.

Female entrepreneurs are over-represented in services and retailing, but there has been a growth in entry into the construction, wholesaling, and transportation sectors. Traditional service sectors are associated with high levels of new firm entry because of their low barriers to entry and lower resources required, as well as high levels of new firm closure. Many of the performance differences between female- and male-owned businesses can, in part, be due to choice of industrial sector rather than real differences between female and male entrepreneurs. Firm performance studies that do not control for industry and resource differences between male- and female-owned businesses

Table 13. Main hurdles reported at work by women

Requisite skills	Sector of activity	Motivation	Management styles	Strategies	Business unit
Limited business skills	Women's choice of smaller, traditional businesses in retail, service, and caring	Different socialization experiences: home and children are the first priority	Relational strategy when working with clients, partners	Limited strategies developed to access resources	Fewer resources at start-up
Limited managerial experience	Women's avoidance of high-tech, manufacturing or non-traditional and too innovative sectors	To cope with the work–family conflict by working independently	Focus on development of teams, employees, empowering, perseverance	Limited strategic and tactical decisions	Focusing on industry-specific experience
Limited entrepreneurial experience	Choice of educational professional tracks that are less rewarding in the labour market	Turning a hobby into a business	Feminine management style, i.e. informally structured	Development of strategies emphasizing product quality; neglecting strategies addressing cost efficiency	Smaller businesses relative to men's

Limited employment of negotiation skills	Just to make a living; I do not necessarily have to be profitable	More work from home, thus less exposure of the business's products or services
Limited employment of financial-management skills		Discrimination—lenders discriminate against women; prefer to lend to established firms, which are usually male dominated

Source: Kariv (2013: 10)

generally find the latter underperforming. However, when industry differences are controlled for, most studies find female-owned businesses perform just as well as those owned by men. Evidence also suggests that when resource differences between male and female entrepreneurs are controlled, female entrepreneurs perform just as well as men on many firm performance indicators, and on some indicators they perform better than men.

Kylie Minogue is a pop princess celebrity who owns a successful business empire through her company Darenote Limited. Her concert tours attract huge crowds and she keeps much more of the revenue generated by ticket sales as opposed to album sales. Kylie's activities illustrate that premium pays. She charges large fees for the exclusivity of giving special invitation-only concerts for hotel openings and VIP or private appearances. Kylie continually focuses on adaptation, change, and diversity. Her endorsements include homewares, perfume (for women and men), books, and clothing. She continually extends her brand by constantly finding new markets in terms of products, services, and location.

Zhang Yin (also known as Cheung Yan) is the 'empress of waste paper', regarded as China's wealthiest person and the wealthiest self-made woman in the world. She is the founder and director of the family company Nine Dragons Paper Holdings, a recycling business that purchases scrap paper from the United States and converts the cardboard into boxes in China, which are then used to export Chinese goods. Whilst working in a Guangdong textile factory, Zhang noticed that the Chinese exporting firms did not have sufficient paper packaging materials. Using personal savings she opened a paper trading company in Hong Kong, which provided a local supply of waste paper. Zhang moved to Los Angeles and with her second husband founded the America Chung Nam paper exporting company, which became the leading US paper exporter. Zhang returned to Hong Kong to co-found

Nine Dragons Paper with her husband and her younger brother, which produces nine million tons of packaging materials per year.

Micro individual perspective and macro business and environment perspective themes explored in female entrepreneurship studies are summarized in Table 14.

Diversity in theoretical underpinnings is exhibited in female entrepreneurship studies. Feminist empiricism, liberal feminist theory, social feminist theory, psychoanalytical feminist theory,

Table 14. Micro and macro perspectives and female entrepreneurship

Micro perspective	Macro perspective
Entrepreneur	*Context*
Personal attributes	Women's role in society
Entrepreneurial characteristics	Inhibiting factors
Motivations	Social networks and social capital
Identity and behaviour	
Prior experience in the labour market	*International setting*
Female-related hurdles and barriers	Perception of female entrepreneurship
Networking	Cultural effect on women's employment
	Necessity-driven vs opportunity-driven environments
Business unit	
Choice of industry	*Public policy issues*
Initial capital resources	Rules, norms, and regulations for female participation in the labour market
Funding strategies	
Investment process	Regulations for mothers; ethnic women entrepreneurs; single mothers, etc.
	Lobby for women entrepreneurs

Source: Kariv (2013: 46)

and radical feminist theory have been used to explore female entrepreneurship.

It is important, however, to bear in mind that female entrepreneurs are not a homogeneous group. There is a need to contextualize and understand different types of female entrepreneur. Robert Goffee and Richard Scase identify the following four patterns of business proprietorship among women relating to the themes of entrepreneurial ideals, and the extent to which they accept conventional gender roles.

Conventional relates to women who are highly committed to entrepreneurial ideals and conventional gender roles. Here women exhibit a subservient gender role, playing a primarily domestic role in supporting their male partner. The motivation is the need to acquire earnings, but the traditional domestic role is retained. Help received from the partner is very limited. *Domestic* relates to women strongly attached to the traditional gender role, but only moderately committed to entrepreneurial ideals. The motivation for business start-up is self-fulfilment. Attachment to the traditional female role limits the development of the business because of the priority attached to the partner and family. *Innovative* women reject the conventional gender role, and are highly committed to entrepreneurial success. This type of female entrepreneur is likely to start businesses in areas where she may have encountered obstacles to her career. *Radical* women regard the business primarily as part of the feminist movement for equality. This type of female entrepreneur has low attachment to both entrepreneurship and conventional gender roles. In these circumstances, the business may be co-owned and operate as a cooperative.

Debate surrounds the wider applicability of this typology of female entrepreneurs, but it highlights the need for academics and practitioners to appreciate diversity in the aspirations, needs, skills, competencies, and knowledge of each type of female entrepreneur. Some of the barriers to entrepreneurship faced by women may not be solely due to gender. Other human capital factors relating to background and experience may be more important.

Customize support to each type of entrepreneur

Differences in types of entrepreneur and firm can lead to diversity in entrepreneurial behaviour and outcomes. Some entrepreneurs generate more substantial job and wealth creation than others. For example, knowledge- and technology-based firms can have a particularly beneficial effect. A driver of efforts to stimulate entrepreneurship is to reduce a dependency culture on the state, and foster choice, opportunity, and personal empowerment, which can reduce social and regional inequality. Policy interventions may involve support initiatives to remove the attitudinal, resource, operational, and strategic barriers to business formation faced by disadvantaged individuals such as disabled people, women, and ethnic minorities. Specifically, support can be designed to help entrepreneurs from these kinds of groups to make economic as well as wider societal contributions. The identification of types of entrepreneur and firm, therefore, has important consequences for national well-being and implications for the design of policy towards entrepreneurs (and firms).

Certain types of entrepreneur or firm may require specific (and customized) types of assistance. Classifications enable practitioners to identify the current goals, resource profiles, strategies, and needs of different types of entrepreneur or firm. These classifications can enable practitioners to provide customized support to each type of entrepreneur or firm, and/or enable them to target support to particular types of entrepreneur or firm who may generate the benefits sought by government and society. For instance, the support required by a portfolio entrepreneur may not be the same as that required by a serial or novice entrepreneur.

In addition, if policymakers want to increase the stock of female entrepreneurs, there may be a case to provide targeted support to females seeking to become self-employed or to start their own business with employees. To encourage more females to enter non-traditional sectors and to own high-growth ventures, there could be a case to address the attitudinal, resource, operational, and strategic barriers to the development of firms owned by female entrepreneurs. Because female entrepreneurs are not homogeneous, there may be a need to provide customized support to different types of female entrepreneur.

Policy implications

The approaches selected to support different types of entrepreneur are largely shaped by the aim of policy. Broad and unfocused policies, that encourage all firms to survive, risk being ineffective if the policy aim is to encourage firm growth. Blanket support to all types of entrepreneur, irrespective of need, ability, and resource profile, may not generate the economic, social, and/or environmental benefits sought by practitioners. Further, blanket policies risk being ineffective if the policy objective is to foster maximum economic development with the minimum amount of public support.

Targeting support to winning firms or entrepreneurs may help maximize the economic returns from publicly subsidized investments (see Chapter 1) and remove market failures faced by entrepreneurs seeking rapid firm growth. Practitioners can adopt a policy of avoiding losers rather than picking winners because the relative losers are easier to identify. The typologies we have been discussing provide practitioners with the entrepreneur and firm profiles to pick winners, avoid losers, or provide customized policy.

The importance of targeting and/or customizing support is illustrated by analysing the assets and liabilities that entrepreneurs accumulate from PBOE. Our research found that apparently greater benefits from PBOE accrue to portfolio entrepreneurs than to serial entrepreneurs. This suggests there could be policy benefits from supporting portfolio entrepreneurs. If the goal of practitioners is to maximize returns from investments, it may be preferable in the short term to target resources to portfolio entrepreneurs who are actively seeking to maximize wealth creation as well as job generation. Such a policy initiative needs to ensure that the private returns to entrepreneurs and their investors are reconciled with social returns. Because serial entrepreneurs seem to be generally less successful than portfolio entrepreneurs, customized schemes could be developed to enable serial entrepreneurs who have owned a previously unsuccessful venture to learn from their prior business ownership failure.

Experienced entrepreneurs also need to be provided with incentives to again engage in entrepreneurial activities. Having created significant personal wealth, some experienced entrepreneurs may be unwilling to risk losing it. As a result, some entrepreneurs could stop being entrepreneurs, or they may become more risk averse in the subsequent ventures they do become involved with. Providing habitual entrepreneurs with financial incentives through changes in the tax regime could encourage them to reinvest profits or funds realized from the sale of a business into subsequent ventures with growth potential.

In addition, customized schemes could seek to hone the entrepreneurial skills of novice entrepreneurs with no PBOE to mobilize. Schemes could foster networking links between inexperienced novice entrepreneurs and successful portfolio entrepreneurs, which will facilitate novice entrepreneurs to accumulate skills, competencies, social capital, etc. These customized schemes would enable novice entrepreneurs to learn from the best business practice of portfolio entrepreneurs. For example, in some universities, academics who have previously

been successful in spinning-out firms based on their research are
encouraged to provide such assistance to more junior colleagues
approaching entrepreneurship for the first time.

Assessing the effects of these more fine-grained policies and using
these findings to inform resource allocation decisions could
usefully inform evaluation of the economic, societal, and
environmental contributions made to local and national
economies by each type of entrepreneur.

Chapter 5
Entrepreneurial thinking and learning

Early research into what made an entrepreneur took the position that an individual's possession of a particular personality trait or particular traits predisposes them towards enterprising behaviour. Several personality traits explored in entrepreneurship studies are summarized in Table 15. However, studies that have attempted to build personality profiles of people who intend to become entrepreneurs, entrepreneurs who have started a business, and entrepreneurs who run successful ventures suggest that entrepreneurs exhibit some, but not all, of the following positive personality traits: risk-taking propensity, strong need for achievement, high tolerance for ambiguity, and or high internal locus of control. We define and discuss below the effectiveness of these traits in identifying entrepreneurs.

Personality approaches

In Chapter 2, we suggested entrepreneurs are risk takers (or risk bearers). Risk taking is dependent on the perception of the situation and/or the decision-maker's perception of being an expert. A person will be risk averse if they perceive themselves to be in a loss situation. However, they will be risk seeking if they perceive themselves to be in a win situation. Individuals who feel competent will also take more risks. People who are older, more

Table 15. Personality trait dimensions in entrepreneurship studies

Personality dimension	Description
Risk-taking propensity	An individual's willingness to pursue decisions or courses of action involving uncertainty regarding success or failure outcomes
Need for achievement	An individual's desire for significant accomplishment, mastering of skills, control, or high standards, and several actions, such as intense, prolonged, and repeated efforts to accomplish something difficult, to work with singleness of purpose towards a high and distant goal, and to have the determination to win
Tolerance of ambiguity	An individual who can deal with ambiguity and uncertainty. People high on tolerance of ambiguity perceive ambiguity of information and behaviour in a neutral and open way, and find complex situations desirable and challenging
Locus of control	Individuals with high internal locus of control believe that they can control events that affect them, that the achievement of a goal is dependent on their own behaviour or individual characteristics, and that an individual's ability, hard work, determination, and planning can enable them to control their own destiny
Conscientiousness	An individual's level of achievement, work motivation, organization and planning, self-control and acceptance of traditional norms, and virtue and responsibility towards others
Openness to experience	An individual who is intellectually curious, imaginative, and creative; someone who seeks out new ideas and alternative values and aesthetic standards

Emotional stability	Individuals who are emotionally stable are described as calm, stable, even-tempered, and are described as hardy, optimistic, and steady in the face of social pressure, stress, and uncertainty. People low on emotional stability (also referred to as high neuroticism) feel vulnerable to psychological stress and experience a range of negative emotions including anxiety and worry, depression, and low self-esteem
Extraversion	People high on extraversion are gregarious, outgoing, warm, and friendly; they are energetic, active, assertive, and dominant in social situations; they experience more positive emotions and are optimistic; and they seek excitement and stimulation
Agreeableness	An individual's attitude toward other people. People high on agreeableness are trusting, altruistic, cooperative, and modest, and show sympathy and concern for the needs of others and tend to defer to others in the face of conflict. People low on agreeableness are manipulative, self-centred, suspicious, and ruthless

Source: Adapted from Delmar (2000) and Zhao et al. (2010)

highly educated, with business experience and longer durations of business experience are generally more risk averse.

Need for achievement (or Nach) espoused by David McClelland is an individual's desire for significant accomplishment, mastering of skills, control, or high standards. A strong need for achievement refers to an individual's preference for success under conditions of competition. People with a strong need for achievement can be distinguished from others as high achievers. Strong need for achievement is linked to several actions, such as intense, prolonged, and repeated efforts to accomplish something difficult, to work with singleness of purpose towards a high and distant goal, and to have the determination to win.

Need for achievement is closely related to risk taking and the difficulty of tasks people choose to undertake. Individuals with a strong need for achievement take into account the perceived risk of the situation and their perceived level of competence. High achievers select situations associated with individual responsibility, personal control over outcomes, moderate risk taking as a function of skill, moderate risk of failure, timely feedback on their performance, knowledge of results of decisions, novel instrumental activity, and anticipation of future possibilities. They prefer striving to achieve moderately difficult targets that are challenging but not beyond their capabilities. The prospect of achievement satisfaction rather than financial gain can promote enterprise behaviour. In contrast, low achievers may select very easy tasks in order to minimize risk of failure, or highly difficult tasks, such that a failure would not be embarrassing. Strong need for achievement is fostered by: parents that encourage independence in childhood; praise and reward as compensation for success; achievement generating positive feelings; and achievement being perceived to be linked to individual competence and effort rather than luck.

Some studies suggest a link between people reporting a strong achievement motivation and an increased probability of becoming an entrepreneur. However, a strong need for achievement may not be the sole or major reason why people engage in enterprising behaviour. Rather, a broader task motivation index that considers the following as distinguishing features of entrepreneurs is more insightful: self-achievement, risk taking, feedback of results, personal innovation, and planning for the future. Indeed, people reporting higher scores on this broader task motivation index report superior business performance. This broader array of factors may work in combination as predictors of successful business entry and performance.

Tolerance of ambiguity is a concept related to risk taking. People high on tolerance of ambiguity perceive ambiguous information and behaviour in a neutral and open way, and find complex situations desirable and challenging. They keep an open mind, have a flexible attitude, focus on the key facts, and are quick to respond to change. Conversely, people with a low tolerance of ambiguity report stress and unpleasantness in complex situations. They generally prefer well-understood situations. In some studies, an individual's propensity to report a high tolerance of ambiguity is linked to the likelihood of becoming an entrepreneur.

Locus of control relates to the extent to which individuals believe that they can control events that affect them. The concept is one of the four dimensions that comprise core self-evaluations relating to self-efficacy, self-esteem, neuroticism, and one's fundamental appraisal of oneself. Julian Rotter suggests that a person's locus can be either internal or external. High internal control relates to where a person believes that the achievement of a goal is dependent on his or her own behaviour or individual characteristics. An individual's ability, hard work, determination, and planning in achieving outcomes may enable them to control their own destiny. People reporting a high internal locus of control believe that they can personally change events in any given situation, and so increase their expectancy of success. External control refers to where a person believes that their environment is beyond their own control, and that some higher power or other people control their decisions and their life. Consequently, they may have a tendency to believe that the achievement of a goal is the result of luck or external factors. Evidence on the role of locus of control is not strong. Some studies show only a low to moderate significant link between people reporting internal control and the propensity to become entrepreneurs. A few studies have detected a weak tendency for people reporting internal control to own superior-performing firms.

More recently, other personality dimensions have been found to be associated with the propensity to become an entrepreneur. Hao Zhao and colleagues detected four personality dimensions, namely conscientiousness that relates to achievement motivation, openness to experience, emotional stability, and extraversion; these were associated with intention to become an entrepreneur and superior entrepreneurial performance. A further personality dimension relating to risk propensity was linked to the intention to become an entrepreneur but not to superior entrepreneurial performance.

While the personality trait approach is intuitively appealing, personality theories do not adequately explain why some individuals engage in entrepreneurial behaviour and others do not. Indeed, studies focusing on entrepreneurs' personality traits have been widely criticized, and have fallen out of favour. As highlighted above, most entrepreneurs do not possess all of the ideal positive personality traits. Further, people who are not entrepreneurs can possess several ideal personality traits.

In addition, biased studies that solely monitor surviving and successful entrepreneurs distort the importance of personality traits. When the personality traits are analysed together, no single dimension turns out to be the most important in shaping the propensity to become an entrepreneur or to achieve superior entrepreneurial performance. In contrast, social context and the entrepreneur's general and specific human capital that we discussed in Chapter 3 are more consistently found to explain whether some people are likely to establish new ventures, particularly those that become very successful.

The theory of planned behaviour developed from the theory of reasoned action presented by Icek Ajzen offers one explanation.

An individual's attitudes and personality traits may have only an indirect impact on specific behaviour. Attitudes and subjective norms, such as perceived behavioural control, rather than personality can promote the intention of individuals to become entrepreneurs and to own superior-performing firms.

A further problem arises because some personality traits that mark out born entrepreneurs are innate and cannot be acquired. Personality traits theories depict general tendencies and neglect the importance of situational factors that may change an individual's behaviour and career choices. Consequently, personality traits theories relate to a static approach that focuses on 'who the entrepreneur is', and not 'what the entrepreneur does'. Bill Gartner's insight that *'Who is an Entrepreneur?' Is the Wrong Question* neatly encapsulates this need to shift to an examination of entrepreneurial behaviour and what influences that behaviour. Psychodynamic and cognitive perspectives present counterpoints to the personality traits approach. It may be easier to change a person's mental processing abilities than their personality.

Psychodynamic approaches

Building upon Sigmund Freud's psychoanalytic theory of personality, psychodynamics have been utilized to explore entrepreneur behaviour. This approach suggests that the socialization process in childhood determines personal attributes, such as instinctive drives, and that some people seek instant gratification for their desires. If instinctive behaviour is severely constrained it can lead to frustration, which may be a source of entrepreneurial motivation.

Drawing on the psychodynamic perspective, Manfred Kets de Vries suggests that entrepreneurial behaviour can be due to negative drives. For Kets de Vries, frustrations and perceived deprivations experienced in the early stages of life shape an individual's personality. Behaviour is explained by experiences related to a troublesome and very disturbed childhood where the father is absent. These individuals are propelled by feelings of poor self-esteem, insecurity, lack of self-confidence, and an inability to fit into an organization. These individuals may be classified as marginal people, or deviants. These individuals search for independence and control to shape their own destiny. Distrust and suspicion of those in positions of authority make it very difficult for them to pursue careers in large, structured organizations. Such individuals may frequently change jobs and potentially gain entrepreneurial experiences in a variety of settings. They may choose high-risk situations and ultimately prefer working for themselves as entrepreneurs.

Kets de Vries suggests that work situations and experiences of people who are not regarded as deviants can also foster negative enterprising behaviour. Individuals can have careers associated with sequences of success(es) and/or failure(s). Some people at an unconscious level fear success (i.e. success is not seen to be deserved) and failure. Due to their frustrations, some people are more likely to exhibit impulsive behaviour and make decisions without careful deliberation. While an entrepreneur's complete immersion in the enterprise can be crucial for initial success, this focus may be exhibited in an autocratic leadership style. This leadership style is associated with a reluctance to delegate and to introduce formal systems, and a propensity to focus on short-term horizons. It can put at risk firm survival and transitions. An entrepreneur can be highly creative and imaginative but also highly rigid and unwilling to change. This perspective questions the view that all entrepreneurs are special people always reporting positive enterprise behaviour (i.e. Schumpeter). In addition, it also stresses the need to explore entrepreneurial behaviour in crisis, failure, and success situations.

A major problem with the psychodynamic approach in drawing general lessons about entrepreneurs is that the findings typically derive from a small number of clinical cases. Deviants are found throughout society. There is no reason to believe that proportionally more become entrepreneurs. Indeed, the evidence is that the majority of entrepreneurs are not drawn from deviant backgrounds. Many entrepreneurs are no more troubled than non-entrepreneurs, and numerous entrepreneurs come from emotionally and financially stable families. Some parents can act as role models, particularly those owning a family business.

The psychodynamic approach does not consider all the situations, stimuli, and barriers (i.e. factors that pull and/or push people into entrepreneurship) that can shape the propensity of people to become entrepreneurs and to own superior-performing firms. Further, it fails to consider lifelong development and the ability of some people to reinvent themselves and deal with earlier failures in life.

Cognitive approaches

An entrepreneur's dominant logic is the information funnel through which their attention is filtered. This information funnel is akin to the entrepreneur's cognition. Cognitive theory is concerned with how incoming information is processed and used. Differences in cognitive processes may explain why people report variations in behaviour and performance. Entrepreneurial cognition studies explore the ways entrepreneurs think and behave compared to non-entrepreneurs, and the knowledge structures used to make assessments, judgements, or decisions involving opportunity evaluation, venture creation, and growth.

Robert Baron found that entrepreneurs are more likely than non-entrepreneurs to experience regret over previously missed opportunities. Entrepreneurs are more likely to search for, identify, and act upon perceived opportunities. They are also more likely to engage in careful, constructive thought. Additionally, entrepreneurs are more likely to experience stronger levels of emotion in relation to their work. They are more prone to their decisions being influenced by affective states unrelated to these decisions, and are more likely to be susceptible to self-serving biases regarding the outcomes of decisions. Baron, however, suggests that more successful entrepreneurs may be less prone to such biases. Successful entrepreneurs are more likely to be overly confident in their predictions about future outcomes and to be more susceptible to escalation of commitment effects in their decision-making.

Lowell Busenitz and Jay Barney showed that entrepreneurs use heuristics more extensively than non-entrepreneurs. Heuristics are rule-of-thumb shortcuts to simplify the contexts for discovering or creating entrepreneurial opportunities, which are often complex, highly uncertain, and lacking in information about the size and profitability of the market for a product that may not yet exist. Entrepreneurs particularly use representativeness and overconfidence, or comparative optimism, heuristics in complex environments where comprehensive assessment of information is not possible. These simplifying heuristics can enable entrepreneurs to make decisions that exploit brief windows of opportunity. This is because heuristic-based information processing has the advantage of speed. Without heuristic-based logic, the discovery, creation, and pursuit of new opportunities may become overwhelming and costly. A reliance on heuristics can reduce the burden of cognitive processing, which can allow the entrepreneur to concentrate on novel or unique material. Definitions of widely used cognitive heuristics and biases dimensions are summarized in Table 16.

Some heuristics can lead to poor decisions. Due to initial overconfidence, decision-makers may be too slow to incorporate additional information about a situation into their assessment. Overconfidence and comparative optimism can encourage an entrepreneur to exploit an opportunity, but they may establish

Table 16. Cognitive heuristics and biases in entrepreneurship

Cognitive dimension	Description
Representativeness	Individual's willingness to generalize from few observations
Overconfidence	Individual is overly optimistic in their initial assessment of a situation (i.e. an unwarranted belief in an individual's abilities to bring about a particular outcome), but are slow to incorporate new information
Over-optimism	An individual's tendency to report that they are less likely than others to experience negative events, and are more likely than others to experience positive events
Availability	Individual is guided by readily available information
Illusion of control	Individual overemphasizes the extent to which their skill can improve performance in situations where chance plays a large role
Anchoring and adjustment	Individual uses a rule of thumb whereby existing information is accepted as a reference point, but it can then be adjusted to take into account various other factors
Conformation bias	Individual's tendency to notice any information that conforms with their views
Planning fallacy	Individual's tendency to underestimate the amount of work and time needed to complete a project
Escalation of commitment	Individual's tendency to stick with decisions that yield negative results even when the negative results continue to mount
Intrinsic motivation	Individual's interest and enjoyment rather than a focus on external reward

(*continued*)

Table 16. Continued

Cognitive dimension	Description
Perceived self-efficacy	Individual's beliefs about their own capabilities to achieve a goal
Success syndrome	A post-success disorder caused by the burdens of having made it
Blind spots	Individual's tendency to see themselves as less biased than other people
Hubris	An individual has lost contact with reality and overestimates their competence or capabilities
Denial	An individual faced with a fact that is too uncomfortable to accept rejects the fact and believes it is not true despite overwhelming evidence
Law of small numbers	Drawing general conclusions from a small number of possibly unrepresentative observations

undercapitalized firms. Undercapitalized firms that overstretch entrepreneurs' actual rather than perceived resources are more susceptible to higher failure rates.

Prior business ownership experience (PBOE)

There is considerable debate about the relationship between entrepreneurial experience and optimism. Some entrepreneurs realize that they were initially too optimistic and subsequently adjust their thinking. Consequently, they report a more realistic outlook in subsequent ventures. Experienced entrepreneurs with PBOE, particularly business failure experience, may be less likely to subsequently report comparative optimism. Alternatively, experienced entrepreneurs may accumulate biases and hence can be subsequently more likely to report comparative optimism.

PBOE offers opportunities to reduce the likelihood of subsequent comparative optimism, but this depends on the nature of the experience. Despite exposure to more learning opportunities through multiple business ownership experiences, habitual entrepreneurs (i.e. PBOE in at least one prior independent firm) not experiencing business failure are more likely than novice entrepreneurs to show comparative optimism. This finding questions the ability of entrepreneurs to learn solely from positive experiences. Some experienced habitual entrepreneurs are prone to the liabilities of success. If there are learning benefits associated with failure, we might anticipate that habitual entrepreneurs who have experienced a business failure would be less likely to show comparative optimism than novice entrepreneurs with no business failure experience. However, only habitual entrepreneurs holding a portfolio of businesses concurrently rather than sequentially (serial entrepreneurs) and who experience business failure are generally less likely than novice entrepreneurs to show comparative optimism.

These results are interesting for two interrelated reasons. First, the pattern of entrepreneurial activity under which business failure is experienced appears to be linked to how the entrepreneur responds to and learns from that experience. Second, there are clear variations amongst the entrepreneurs who have experienced business failure. Entrepreneurs who have experienced business failure should not be aggregated into a single crude business failure group, which does not differentiate economic business failure from failure to meet an entrepreneur's expectations.

The emotional costs of business failure can be 'diluted' for portfolio entrepreneurs because they have another business or other businesses to fall back on. Portfolio entrepreneurs could adopt an experimental approach and diversify their risk by making smaller and incremental investments into two or more new ventures at the same time. They could strategically seek to minimize the emotional and financial costs of business failure. In contrast to serial entrepreneurs, portfolio entrepreneurs may be more able to distance themselves from their ventures and adopt a more objective evaluation of each business owned.

Motivation and self-efficacy

Intrinsic motivation concerns an individual's representation of what they find enjoyable and fulfilling. Intrinsically motivated behaviour may have no apparent financial reward, but it helps shape emotions, attitudes, and goals. It can also subsequently shape an entrepreneur's ability to be creative, their attraction to challenges, and the ability to search for information to discover and exploit an opportunity. Intrinsic motivation may, in addition, mean that entrepreneurs with a high level of interest in their commercial activities will experience a higher feeling of enjoyment and have superior decision-making abilities. Conversely, extrinsic motivation relates to individual behaviour that is influenced by external motivators such as financial reward rather than interest in the task itself. Intrinsic motivation is closely related to high self-efficacy.

Linked to the concept of locus of control is the concept of perceived self-efficacy. Albert Bandura showed that people with high levels of perceived self-efficacy have assurance in their own capabilities to report subsequent attainments. They are motivated individuals seeking to control events in their lives.

People with a high level of self-efficacy approach difficult tasks as challenges to be mastered rather than issues to be avoided. On the other hand, people with a low self-efficacy shy away from difficult tasks, which are perceived as personal threats. Individuals with high levels of self-efficacy maintain a strong commitment to achieving difficult goals and persisting with them even in the face of failure. They also tend to attribute failure to insufficient effort and poor knowledge. In contrast, individuals with low self-efficacy have a low level of aspiration and commitment to their chosen goals, do not maintain any analytical focus, and give up easily. Failure is attributed to external obstacles and personal deficiencies. As a consequence they rapidly lose faith in their own capabilities. A person's level of self-efficacy is often the result of previous successful or unsuccessful experiences (either personal experiences or those of role models). Therefore self-efficacy will tend to create a virtuous or vicious circle, where on the one hand success breeds success but on the other failure breeds failure.

People reporting high levels of perceived self-efficacy are indeed generally more likely to establish new firms and to explore new opportunities. In any given situation, entrepreneurs tend to perceive more opportunities than non-entrepreneurs, who usually perceive the same situation to have more costs and greater risks. Some people avoid entrepreneurial activities not because they lack ability but because they believe that they do not have such ability. However, people reporting high levels of perceived self-efficacy are not markedly more likely to report an intention to grow their firms.

Assets and liabilities of experience

Experience can shape an individual's cognition. Habitual entrepreneurs may learn from the feedback from their PBOE to adjust their judgement when they come to consider exploiting a subsequent opportunity. By evaluating carefully the feedback from earlier firms owned, habitual entrepreneurs can create a dynamic cycle of learning. This PBOE may enhance their capacity to acquire and organize the complex but incomplete information relating to a new entrepreneurial opportunity. As highly experienced decision-makers, they should be in a better position to manipulate this information into recognizable patterns that form the basis for entrepreneurial actions. Because habitual entrepreneurs have multiple experiences to draw upon, they can be more likely to process information about potential new opportunities using heuristics than novice entrepreneurs with no PBOE. Novice entrepreneurs may have fewer experience-related mental shortcuts to draw upon. Rather, these inexperienced individuals are more likely to adopt more analytical or systematic information processing styles.

Experience-based knowledge can change how entrepreneurs think, and can lead habitual entrepreneurs to greater creativity in formulating and exploiting subsequent opportunities. However, the downside is that habitual entrepreneurs' over-reliance on heuristics may mean that they continue to adopt decision-making processes that are not appropriate in new situations, especially in changing environments. As a result, some habitual entrepreneurs can be prone to the biases associated with heuristic decision-making. Entrepreneurial experience may then lead to negative as well as positive learning outcomes.

For example, some experienced entrepreneurs may think that they already know enough about a particular context for a new opportunity. They can infer too much from the limited information available because they want to confirm prior beliefs. As warned above, some experienced entrepreneurs may become constrained by sticking with what is familiar to them and become overconfident in their judgements, even though the new context is different.

Entrepreneurs who are utilizing what they have learnt from their past experiences can find it becomes harder to recognize industry, technology, regulatory, or market changes. Instead of adapting heuristics that worked in the past to the new context, they may attempt to repeat the same recipes, with fairly predictable consequences. This liability of staleness arising from a feeling that they know how things are done can retard an entrepreneur's ability to identify new business opportunities and/or to develop strategies to exploit new opportunities.

Some habitual entrepreneurs can continue to focus upon interpersonal relationships used in the past. They may employ existing resources and knowledge in the new firm, thereby reducing the tendency to acquire context-relevant resources. This liability of sameness can hinder their ability to change, or to adapt to changing external environmental conditions. The latter entrepreneurs may not be able to adjust their interaction and learning patterns to the demands of their new firm. These accumulated liabilities help explain why the performance of a subsequent venture owned by a habitual entrepreneur can be below that of their first venture (or may simply not be higher than the first if assets offset liabilities).

Kamran Elahian, who co-founded the highly successful Cirrus Logic semiconductor company, is a case in point. He subsequently went on to found the pen-based computer company Momenta Corporation but was fired as chairman as the company collapsed. Kamran Elahian is reported as saying that he was too sure of his own infallibility to see clearly the software problems, lack of market readiness for the product, and excessive marketing expenditure.

Failure experience

But the impact on learning from PBOE may be largely influenced by whether that experience involved a successful or an economic business failure (i.e. firm bankruptcy) and/or a non-economic business failure (i.e. the venture closed because its performance was too low in relation to the entrepreneur's expectations). Dealing with failure is an important attribute of entrepreneurs. There is a distinction between failure and intelligent failure. Entrepreneurs may learn more from intelligent failure involving modest failures that were large enough to generate entrepreneur attention but not too large to generate negative responses.

Some habitual entrepreneurs can become demotivated. Previously successful habitual entrepreneurs may not put the same amount of effort and risk taking into running a subsequent firm. This is because they have now amassed significant personal wealth. Previous success may also result in the success syndrome, illusion of control, blind spots, and overconfidence. Some habitual entrepreneurs who have not accumulated sufficient resources may have neither the ability nor the flexibility to choose appropriate opportunities a second time.

Habitual entrepreneurs who have previously failed can be in denial. If they have been emotionally closely involved with a business that fails they may experience loss resembling grief that precludes them from moving on and learning from the situation. Dean Shepherd, a professor of entrepreneurship at Indiana University, recounts the example of his father's reaction to the failure of the family firm:

> When our family business died, my father exhibited a number of worrying emotions. There was numbness and disbelief that this business he had created twenty odd years ago was no longer 'alive'. There was some anger toward the economy, competitors, and debtors. A stronger emotion than anger was that of guilt and self-blame: he felt guilty that he had caused the failure of the business, that it could no longer be passed on to my brother, and that, as a result, he had failed not only as a businessperson but also as a father. These feelings caused him distress and anxiety. He felt the situation was hopeless and became withdrawn and, at times, depressed. (Shepherd, 2003)

Entrepreneurs who have experienced business failure but return to subsequent business ownership may become more risk averse and less innovative because of fear of a further failure. On the other hand, if an entrepreneur deliberately closes or reconfigures a business that has failed to meet their expectations, the learning process from this kind of failure can be more positive. Learning from entrepreneurial failure could also be related to prior patterns of success and/or failure. If failure of one business is an isolated case among a series of successes, or among a portfolio of ventures, it may weigh less heavily in the entrepreneur's cognitive processes.

The value of experience, therefore, depends not just on the knowledge gained but also on how this knowledge is subsequently used. Mindful use of prior experience is required. Entrepreneurs need to recognize when it is necessary to switch away from heuristic information processing toward more systematic information processing to guide decision-making. Experts can demonstrate a greater awareness of the level of uncertainty involved in opportunity identification, and they are able to match their cognitive processes to the task in hand. Experienced habitual entrepreneurs have the potential to become expert entrepreneurs, yet experience is a necessary but not a sufficient condition for becoming an expert.

We do not know a great deal about the wider applicability of cognitive theories relating to the behaviour of entrepreneurs outside closed experimental settings. There are very few systematic studies involving representative samples of real entrepreneurs reporting actual rather than potential behaviour scenarios. In addition, we have no clear and consistent evidence on which specific cognitive skills need to be accumulated and mobilized by individuals at alternative points along the entrepreneurial process. We do not know whether all entrepreneurs that learn from failure become better entrepreneurs. This is an important theme. Policies aimed at incentivizing all failed entrepreneurs to re-enter business ownership on the grounds that they will have learnt from their experience could be too simplistic. What is also missing from our knowledge about entrepreneurial behaviour is that, although many entrepreneurial ventures are founded by teams, we know little about how these teams collectively use shared mental models or cognition to decide whether and how to exploit a subsequent entrepreneurial opportunity.

Chapter 6
Forms of entrepreneurial venture

Considerable attention on entrepreneurship focuses on the creation of a new business, but this seriously underestimates the wider extent of entrepreneurial activity. Besides start-ups, the discovery, creation, and exploitation of opportunities can take place within family firms, established corporations, and other organizations. Changes in organizational structures and processes in family and large corporations can facilitate entrepreneurship where it was not possible before. Entrepreneurial activities of family firms can be reinvigorated by a change in generational leadership. In some cases for entrepreneurship to flourish there may need to be mobility of an activity from its current owners to a new ownership regime, such as in management buyouts and academic spin-offs. Entrepreneurship may, in addition, take the form of a social enterprise where the objective is to maximize the amount of social value created whilst also attaining its financial goals.

Family firms

Enterprising skills and knowledge can be accumulated in first-generation family-owned firms. This pool of entrepreneurial knowledge could be transferred (and enriched) in second- or subsequent-generation family-owned firms. Indeed, for family firms to continue over generations they may need to revitalize or even change from their initial entrepreneurial activities. The size and contribution of family firms to the economy are significant. But the amount varies according to how they are defined, which can relate to perception of family kinship ties, majority family ownership, majority family management, and intergenerational transition to a second or later generation of family members. Family members can be involved in the ownership and or management of the firm, creating three interdependent subsystems of family, ownership, and management. A major challenge for the survival and entrepreneurial direction of family firms is due to the intertwining of family and business objectives. Advantages and disadvantages of family firms are summarized in Table 17.

Family firms may begin by being entrepreneurial but some find this hard to sustain. For example, Linn is a second-generation family-owned firm based in Scotland that produces innovative hi-fi systems. The company has a long-term vision to enrich people's lives through music, of being an integrated manufacturer employing people in the local area, and it seeks to create valuable jobs that contribute to society. In a fast-changing industry, continuous innovation is important and survival of the company into the second generation depends on repositioning the company and on prudent management.

Family firm owners focusing on wealth creation and business development may prefer to recruit non-family professional managers. The Warburtons bakery established in Lancashire in England has been a family-owned business for five generations. Family members still hold senior management positions. With regard to the last two generations of family ownership, the firm has employed senior non-family executives to assist firm growth and prosperity. In May 2006, a non-family member took over as the managing director. Some family member owners recognize that the family's interests are best served by bringing in the best people, and family members are surrounded by people (i.e. outsiders) who are better at their jobs than family members.

Table 17. Advantages and disadvantages of family firms

Advantages	Disadvantages

Private family-owned firms

Advantages	Disadvantages

• *Goals*
  - independent family firm survival
  - transfer firm to next generation of family
  - long-term investments
	• *Goals*
	  - relationship based and not solely a performance system
	  - protect family agendas over business agendas
	  - maintain/enhance lifestyle of family owners

• *Ownership*
  - maximize family income
  - provide jobs for family members
	• *Ownership*
	  - less emphasis on immediate profitability
	  - reluctance to sell equity to outsiders
	  - aversion to debt can constrain growth

• *Management*
  - family knowledge and employ family
  - family ties; stability, loyalty, and trust
	• *Management*
	  - kinship rather than ability shapes managerial positions
	  - reluctant to use expertise of outsiders
	  - management introverted, inflexible, and dated

• *Strategy*
  - product quality
  - quality service for customer loyalty
  - use formalized management systems
	• *Strategy*
	  - repeat established strategies that worked well in the past
	  - prefer not to focus on creativity and innovation
	  - reluctance to discover new opportunities

Private and public family-controlled businesses

Advantages	Disadvantages
• Long-term orientation	• Less access to capital markets may curtail growth

• Greater independence of action
  - less (or no) pressure from stock market
  - less (or no) takeover risk
	• Confusing organization
	  - messy structure
	  - no clear division of tasks

• Family culture as a source of pride
  - stability
	• Nepotism
	  - tolerance of inept family members as managers

- strong identification/
  commitment/motivation
- continuity in leadership
- Greater resilience in hard
  times
  - willing to plough back
    profits
- Less bureaucratic and
  impersonal
  - greater flexibility
  - quicker decision-making
- Financial benefits
  - possibility of great success
- Knowing the business
  - early training for family
    members

- inequitable reward system
- greater difficulties in
  attracting professional
  management
- Spoiled kid syndrome
- Internecine strife
  - family disputes overflow into
    the business
- Paternalistic/autocratic rule
  - resistance to change
  - secrecy
  - attraction of dependent
    personalities
- Financial strain
  - family members milking the
    business
  - disequilibrium between
    contribution and
    compensation
- Succession dramas

Source: Adapted from Kets de Vries (1993: 61), Westhead (1997), Westhead and Cowling (1997), and Westhead et al. (1997)

Only about one-third of family firms survive to the second generation, and around 10 per cent make it to the third generation. Family firm first-generation succession involves the process of passing of the leadership baton from the founder-owner to the successor who will be either a family member or a non-family member. The intertwined systems of family, management, and ownership mean that the succession decision involves both strategic and family issues.

The choice of successor is critical as it affects family relationships and the long-term direction of the business. Some children do not want to join the family business because they prefer to establish their own independent firms or careers. They may have entrepreneurial ideas but perceive that a dominant founder or interference from family shareholders not involved in managing the business will constrain their ability to pursue new opportunities which could, in fact, be needed to ensure the longer-term survival of the business. A major problem is that many family firms fail to plan for succession, with less than half reporting that they have a succession plan. Barriers to succession planning are summarized in Table 18.

Succession transitions in family firms can take place in three main ways. First, the senior leadership may be replaced without changing the fundamental form of the business. Second, the authority and control structure can be changed from a simple form to an increasingly complex one, such as changing from one controlling owner to a sibling partnership. Third, devolutionary successions move the system to a simpler form, such as from a cousin consortium to a sibling partnership.

J. Barbour and Sons Ltd designs, manufactures, and markets clothing for men, women, and children under the Barbour brand. In 1894, John Barbour established an oilcloth importing business in South Shields, England. The firm became well known for its waxed cotton outdoor jackets. These are so well known that some

Table 18. Barriers to succession planning in family firms

Founder/owner	Family
• Death anxiety	• Death as taboo
• Company as symbol	- Discussion is a hostile act
- Loss of identity	- Fear of loss/abandonment
- Concern about legacy	• Fear of sibling rivalry
• Dilemma of choice	• Change of spouse's position
- Fiction of equality	
• Generational envy	
- Loss of power	

Source: Adapted from Kets de Vries (1993: 68)

people refer to any waxed cotton jacket as a 'Barbour jacket,' irrespective of manufacturer. Today this fifth-generation business remains headquartered in the north-east of England. Barbour continues to be wholly family owned. Unlike many family firms when it comes to succession, gender has never been an issue. A woman first shared the reins back in 1939 at a time when women appeared in the boardroom only if they were pushing a tea trolley. Operating as a family business and retaining complete control over decision-making have allowed Barbour to make such radical choices, and to respond rapidly to market changes. Dame Margaret Barbour is the chairman and her daughter, Helen, is the company's vice-president. The firm focuses on rejuvenation and new markets. Barbour has been innovative in entering the 'waterproof breathable' market with its own type of waterproof liners, cordura external fabric, and polar fleece sweaters. The firm also focuses on branding and marketing a diverse array of premium products to people engaged in country pursuits. The firm has royal warrants from HM Queen Elizabeth II, HRH Duke of Edinburgh, and HRH The Prince of Wales.

Family firms are not homogeneous. Heterogeneity may affect the nature of business development and the design of sustainability initiatives. Differences in the nature of ownership, management structures, and objectives give rise to six principal family firm types, which are illustrated in Figure 6. Ownership ranges from close family ownership, diluted ownership within the family, and diluted ownership outside the family (i.e. the vertical axis). Family firms' management varies from family dominated through to non-family dominated (i.e. the horizontal axis). Objectives range from financial objectives to family or non-financial objectives that focus on maintaining the longer-term stewardship of the business, or what has been termed the socio-emotional wealth of the family (i.e. the diagonal arrow).

While the average family firm emphasizes family objectives and has closely held family ownership and family management,

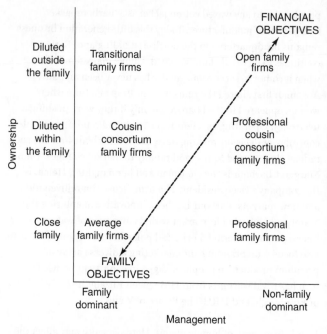

FINANCIAL OBJECTIVES

Diluted outside the family — Transitional family firms — Open family firms

Ownership

Diluted within the family — Cousin consortium family firms — Professional cousin consortium family firms

Close family — Average family firms — Professional family firms

FAMILY OBJECTIVES

Family dominant — Non-family dominant

Management

6. Conceptualized types of family firm

professional family firms report a mix of family and non-family objectives, but emphasize family objectives. Cousin consortium family firms involve a mix of family and non-family objectives with ownership diluted within the family and management dominated by family members. In contrast, professional cousin consortium family firms have diluted within family ownership and management dominated by non-family members. This type of family firm tends to place more emphasis on financial objectives than cousin consortium family firms. Transitional family firms report both family and non-family objectives, but place greater emphasis on financial objectives. Ownership may be diluted outside the family but family members dominate management. These firms are transitional because the management is expected to move towards less family dominance. Finally, open family firms focus on financial objectives. They have diluted ownership outside the family and non-family management is dominant.

Corporate entrepreneurship

Corporate entrepreneurship (CE) is the process whereby an individual or a group of individuals, in association with an existing organization, create a new organization or instigate renewal or innovation within that organization. It can arise as a mix of responses to (anticipated) changes in an existing organization's market environment, and proactive entrepreneurial discovery of new opportunities by people working in the organization, facilitated by organizational structures that encourage entrepreneurial behaviour. In Table 19, CE terminology is summarized.

The renewal activities embodied in CE enhance an organization's ability to compete and take risks, possibly through the addition of new businesses, and the disposal of some existing ones. Strategic renewal refers to the corporate entrepreneurial efforts that result in significant changes to an organization's business or corporate-level strategy or structure. In most cases, this will involve some sort of innovation. This aspect of CE relates to strategic entrepreneurship (see Chapter 3).

Corporate venturing also focuses on the processes associated with creating new businesses, and integrating them into the firm's overall business portfolio. The new business organizations may follow from or lead to innovations that exploit new markets or new product offerings, or both. These venturing efforts could result in the formation of new divisions. Corporate venturing provides organizations with the opportunity to assess new technologies and markets at a relatively early stage in their development.

Table 19. Corporate entrepreneurship terminology

Terms	Unique criteria
Corporate entrepreneurship	Organizational creation, renewal, or innovation + instigated by an existing organizational entity
Strategic renewal/strategic entrepreneurship	Organizational renewal involving major strategic and/or structural changes + instigated by an existing organizational entity + resides within existing organizational domain
Corporate venturing	Organizational creation + instigated by an existing organizational entity + treated as a new business
External corporate venturing	Organizational creation + instigated by an existing organizational entity + treated as new businesses + resides outside existing organizational domain
Internal corporate venturing	Organizational creation + instigated by an existing organizational entity + treated as new business + resides within existing organizational domain
Dimensions of internal corporate venturing	1. Structural autonomy 2. Relatedness to existing business(es) 3. Extent of innovation 4. Nature of sponsorship

Source: Adapted from Sharma and Chrisman (1999: 21)

External corporate venturing refers to corporate venturing activities that lead to the creation of semi-autonomous or autonomous organizational entities, which to varying degrees reside outside the existing corporation. Examples are corporate ventures that are formed due to joint ventures, spin-offs, and corporate VC initiatives. Internal corporate venturing relates to the creation of new businesses that generally reside within the corporate structure, although they may be located outside the organization as semi-autonomous entities, such as spin-offs.

Direct corporate venturing involves direct investment in new ventures that can be subsidiaries of the corporation, spin-offs, or independent entities. Indirect corporate venturing concerns investment by corporations in VC funds, which in turn are invested in new ventures. The indirect approach provides contacts and access to ventures that may be worth investing in, whilst the direct approach may enhance specific business relationships.

Jeff Covin and Morgan Miles distinguish between sustained regeneration, organizational regeneration, strategic renewal, and domain redefinition to generate competitive advantage for firms. These are summarized in Table 20.

Firms that regularly and continuously introduce new products or services or enter new markets exhibit sustained regeneration. These firms have cultures, structures, and systems supportive of innovation and continually cull older products and services in an effort to improve overall competitiveness. They seek to sustain or improve their competitive standing by altering internal processes, structures, and capabilities.

Firms exhibiting strategic renewal seek to redefine their relationships with markets or industry competitors by deliberate major repositioning that better enables resource use to exploit market opportunities. These firms may proactively create a new product market arena that others have not recognized, or they may actively seek to exhibit domain redefinition. Products introduced are innovative from the perspective of the firm, the industry, and the market. The firm takes the competition to a new arena where its first or early mover status creates the basis for sustainable competitive advantage. Further, the firm creates an

Table 20. Corporate entrepreneurship (CE) attributes

Form of CE	Focus of CE	Typical basis for competitive advantage	Typical frequency of form of CE*	Magnitude of entrepreneurship negative impact if entrepreneurial act is unsuccessful
Sustained regeneration	New products or new markets	Differentiation	High frequency	Low
Organizational rejuvenation	The organization	Cost leadership	Moderate frequency	Low to moderate
Strategic renewal	Business strategy	Varies with specific form manifestation	Less frequent	Moderate to high
Domain redefinition	Creation and exploitation of product market arenas	Quick response	Infrequent	Varies with specific form of manifestation and contextual consideration

Notes: * CE actions include the following for: Sustained regeneration: a new product introduction or the entrance of a new to the firm but existing market; Organizational rejuvenation: a major, internally focused innovation aimed at improving firm functioning or strategy implementation; Strategic renewal: the pursuit of a new strategic direction; Domain redefinition: the creation and exploitation of a new, previously unoccupied product market arena

Source: Covin and Miles (1999: 57)

industry standard or defines the benchmark against which later entrants are judged.

Bypass strategies to avoid competitive confrontation in a specific product market arena are a form of domain redefinition, and help decrease overall vulnerability to adverse current competitive conditions. Product market pioneering domain redefinition can redefine a firm's product market domains or product categories.

Management buyouts

Over the past two decades, a new mode of entrepreneurship has spread worldwide involving change in the ownership of existing businesses. In general, management buyouts involve the creation of a new independent entity in which ownership is concentrated in the hands of management and private equity (PE) firms, if present, with substantial funding provided by banks. PE firms become active investors through taking board seats and specifying contractual restrictions on the behaviour of management that include detailed reporting requirements.

Buyouts can take several forms. A *leveraged buyout* (LBO) or investor-led buyout (IBO) is typically a publicly quoted corporation or a large division of a group, which is acquired by a specialist PE firm. The PE firm will typically either retain existing management to run the company or bring in new management to do so, or employ some combination of internal and external management. Incumbent management may or may not receive a direct equity stake or may receive stock options. In the United States, the resulting private company is typically controlled by a small board of directors representing the PE firm, with the chief executive officer (CEO) usually the only insider on the board.

A *management buyout* (MBO) usually involves the acquisition of a divested division or subsidiary or of a private family-owned firm by a new company in which the existing management takes a substantial proportion of the equity, especially in smaller transactions. MBOs typically involve a small group of senior managers as equity holders.

A *management buy-in* (MBI) is simply an MBO in which the leading members of the management team are outsiders. Although superficially similar to MBOs, MBIs carry greater risks as incoming management do not have the benefits of the insiders' knowledge of the operation of the business. Hybrid buy-in/buyouts (so-called BIMBOs) can obtain the benefits of the entrepreneurial expertise of the outside managers and the intimate internal knowledge of the incumbent management.

Traditionally, buyouts were associated with refocusing the strategic activities of underperforming listed corporations. For example, the high-profile dismemberment of RJR-Nabisco gave rise to the actions of investors being seen as barbarians at the gate. In the first wave of buyouts in the 1980s and the second wave in the first decade of this century, these controversial activities were viewed by unions and some policy circles as the 'strip it, flip it' approach, where new owners sell off the valuable assets and quickly exit the business. Evidence shows that this is a misleading view of buyouts. Buyouts can result in two types of entrepreneurial actions that contribute to wealth creation. First, reconfiguring the way in which the buyout operates creates new combinations that lead to more efficient use of resources. Second, the new incentive structure from managerial equity ownership and freedom from head office constraints can lead to the pursuit of new entrepreneurial opportunities.

Four principal types of buyout are illustrated in Table 21.

Control and incentive mechanisms typically used in buyouts may produce enhancements to efficiency. These firms are labelled *efficiency buyouts* (Quadrant 1). The incentives enabled by the introduction of significant managerial equity ownership, the

Table 21. Typology of buyouts

	Individual mindset	
	Managerial mindset	**Entrepreneurial mindset**
- Pre-buyout context and decision mindset	Quadrant 1: Efficiency buyout	Quadrant 4: Buyout failure
	Agency problems; low risk. Decisions based primarily on systematic data and financial criteria	Mismatch of mindset, incentives, and governance
	Post buyout: high leverage and financial control	Post buyout: high leverage and financial control
- Pre-buyout context and decision mindset	Quadrant 2: Revitalization buyout	Quadrant 3: Entrepreneurial buyout
	Bureaucratic procedures stifle innovation and investment needed to be competitive; moderate risk. Decisions to renew competitive capabilities via innovations are based on their already proven success among key competitors	Bureaucratic procedures stifle radical innovations associated with uncertainty and limited information; or technology-based businesses headed in the wrong direction; high risk. Heuristic-based logic can lead to strategic innovations and efficient decision-making
	Post buyout: flexible leverage and financial monitoring by private equity firms	Post buyout: flexible leverage; financial monitoring and technical skills of private equity firms

Source: Adapted from Wright et al. (2000)

pressure to perform in order to service interest payments introduced by the high leverage taken on to acquire the business, and the active monitoring by PE firms all contribute to reducing agency problems in mature firms with significant cash flows that would otherwise be wasted on inefficient diversification. Executives with a managerial mindset are expected to respond positively to enhanced monetary incentives by improving efficiencies.

In large, integrated diverse organizations, bureaucratic measures may be adopted to try to ensure performance. These measures can restrict experimentation and constrain innovative activity. These problems may be eased after the buyout. Instead of following headquarters' controls designed to optimize the goals of the diversified parent company but which block innovation and investment, the buyout creates discretionary power for the new management team to decide what is best for the business. Limited or incremental innovation will result if the new owner-managers possess only managerial cognition. The latter firms are labelled *revitalization buyouts* (Quadrant 2).

Management with an entrepreneurial cognition or mindset, which adopts heuristic-based decision-making (see Chapter 5), may be able to pursue entrepreneurial opportunities that it had discovered but which could not previously be pursued within a larger group. For example, entrepreneurial buyouts can emerge in technology-based industries where the parent did not have the capability to manage or understand the technology but where divisional management does. This subset of buyouts is labelled *entrepreneurial buyouts* (Quadrant 3). These entrepreneurial buyouts require management with superior and idiosyncratic skills to process limited and incomplete information on new opportunities, rather than managers who respond well to close monitoring to prevent them not putting in the full effort to meet shareholders' interests (i.e. shirking). Studies of management's motivation for buying out show the importance of being able to develop strategic opportunities that could not be carried out under the previous owners, and to control their own destiny. For example, the management of the clothing retailer Kohl's bought out the company from the large conglomerate BAT and introduced numerous innovations including new store design, and transformed the company into a discounter/department store hybrid.

Entrepreneurial owner-managers can have the skills and incentives to pursue strategic innovations; but as a new venture, little control may have been exercised over management even when the firm has grown sufficiently to achieve an initial public offering (IPO) on a stock market. When a firm in such circumstances encounters financial difficulties, a buyout opportunity may arise to introduce necessary governance mechanisms, which will allow the innovative opportunities to continue to be exploited, but in a more effectively controlled way. The latter entrepreneurial buyouts are labelled *busted tech buyouts*. For example, in the United States the troubled disk drive company Seagate Technology was initially taken private from its public listing in 2000. This was to enable the company to restructure and develop new innovative products with higher margins away from the short-term demands of the stock market. By 2002, the company successfully returned to the stock market, and by August 2003 was named the number one company for innovation and enterprise in disk drives by *VARBusiness* magazine.

To facilitate the development of more entrepreneurial buyouts, firms may require a level of leverage that is below the norm for buyouts in mature sectors, and a PE firm that has more innovative skills than has traditionally been associated with buyouts. This approach allows for the extension of the PE-backed buyout concept to more innovative, growth-oriented sectors. Where a mismatch occurs between the availability of opportunities, the governance structure, and the managerial mindset, a *buyout failure* occurs (Quadrant 4).

A buyout can ensure survival of a family firm. All or the majority of the ordinary voting shares in the former private family firm can be bought by former managers who had no family ties with the former owners. An MBO may preserve the identity and culture of the (former) family firm, and the psychic income (i.e. the intrinsic reward from being associated with the family firm) of the former family owners can be maintained if they secure continuing involvement in the family firm buyout (i.e. networking links with established suppliers, customers, etc.). Non-family managers have the ability to discover and exploit growth opportunities that could have been resisted before the buyout by former family firm owners who may have been more interested in family lifestyle agendas rather than agendas focused on improving efficiency and profitability. In some cases, where dominant family owners have developed strong second-tier management, a pool of managerial talent located outside the family firm may be required to purchase the family firm via an MBI in order to take advantage of entrepreneurial opportunities that were being missed.

Academic spin-offs

So far, we have focused on entrepreneurial activities emanating from a commercial context. But increasingly, the traditionally non-commercial context of a university provides scope to create spin-off firms to transfer inventions from the laboratory to the marketplace.

A cornerstone of enterprise policy is the promotion of innovative new firms that can play a key role in enhancing economic growth. The new-technology-based firms (NTBFs) created by academics that have spun off from universities and research institutes are attracting worldwide attention as a potential new source of entrepreneurship, which can make a major contribution to growth and economic development. This development has been driven by decreases in public funding for research at universities, a growing public debate about the role of universities in society, and legislative changes regarding the ownership and exploitation of intellectual property (IP) created in universities. Universities target the creation of spin-off firms by academics, in which both the university and the academics hold equity stakes, in the belief that these firms will create significant profit streams and capital gains when they are sold. The expectation is that the returns from spin-off firms will exceed the returns from more traditional licensing agreements and contract research. However, there is debate about whether this is in fact the case, or whether universities have been successful at creating spin-offs with significant capital gains potential. The case of Renovo in Chapter 3 provides an example of an academic spin-off.

Narrowly defined, academic spin-offs relate to new ventures dependent upon licensing or the assignment of a university's IP for initiation. A university may own equity in the spin-off in return for the patent rights it has assigned, or in lieu of licence fees. A substantial proportion of spin-off firms from universities do not build upon formal codified IP, and they do not involve equity stakes held by universities. The latter start-ups by university faculties draw on the individual's own IP or knowledge. To some extent academics have for many years created such ventures. Recent developments by university employers have attempted to limit, if not eliminate, these informal ventures. The relative importance of spin-off firms that involve formal IP and those that do not depends upon the research composition at the university, the country context (i.e. in some countries the IP belongs to the scientist, not the university), university policy regarding IP rights, or the entrepreneurial activity of the academics themselves.

NTBFs can also be created by graduates after they have left the university, or by outsiders who draw on IP created by universities. Although there are likely to be substantial numbers of these kinds of NTBFs, it is usually unclear whether these start-ups can be linked to specific knowledge created and transferred in the university setting, or whether they are based on knowledge that the graduate cumulated outside the university.

Academics creating spin-off firms have several options open to them. They may leave the university to devote themselves completely to the spin-off firm. Alternatively, they may remain with the university and work with the venture part-time. Whether great academic scientists are able to transform into great entrepreneurs is a moot point given their traditionally non-commercial background. Bringing in a surrogate (external) entrepreneur with commercial experience can provide the missing entrepreneurial input to enable the innovation to be developed from the laboratory to a viable product in the marketplace. A combination of academic and surrogate entrepreneurs in the board of the new company may enable universities to simultaneously exploit the technical benefits of inventor involvement and the commercial know-how of surrogate entrepreneurs.

Academic spin-off firms differ in their ability to generate significant capital gains. Table 22 illustrates that the nature of support provided by universities to spin-offs varies, which can shape venture development. Mike Wright and colleagues made a distinction between VC-backed type (10 per cent of spin-offs), prospector type (50 per cent), and lifestyle type (40 per cent).

The *VC-backed type* is probably the most attractive from a policy perspective. These firms have technology that has the potential to create large new markets and with a capital gain likely to be realized through a stock market flotation (i.e. IPO), or sale to an established multinational corporation. Significant VC backing is sought in the early stages to develop the technology into products that will subsequently generate revenue. In many cases, these ventures may not have generated revenue streams from their products (apart from consultancy income) prior to their IPO, because of the extremely long lead times and high risk in their development through various stages of clinical trials and regulatory approval. These spin-offs must be able to attract most of the researchers that were working on the technology at the university to retain scientific credibility. Most universities are likely to have very few research groups with world-leading research capable of generating this kind of spin-off.

Many academic spin-offs have limited potential and are labelled *prospector types*. The technology base underpinning their founding is generally not sufficiently novel to generate radically

Table 22. Types of academic spin-off

		Venture capital-backed type	Prospector type	Lifestyle type
Institutional link	Formal involvement	Equity relation based upon a complex IP system	Equity relations based upon one patent or none	Licence, contract, informal relations
	Prestige of research group	Worldwide recognition in a broad domain	Worldwide recognition in a focused subdomain or local recognition	Various
Business model	Investor vs market acceptance	Investor acceptance	Both Investor and market acceptance	Market acceptance
	Mode of value capturing	Clear IP-maximizing strategy or value chain acquisition Strategy to prepare trade sale/IPO	Optimize time to break even and future trade sale value, no clear exit yet	Optimize profit
Technology resources	Degree of innovativeness	Disruptive technology or market	New product based upon non-disruptive technology	New product/service addresses clear unmet market need
	Stage of product/service development	Early, sometimes not even defined	Early (alpha) prototype	Almost market-ready product/service
	Broadness of the technology concept	Can be broad	Narrow	Not relevant

(continued)

Table 22. Continued

		Venture capital-backed type	Prospector type	Lifestyle type
Financial resources	*VC involvement*	Able to attract €1–5 million in the first 18 months after founding	Lower amount of business angels, baby venture capital, or public fund kind of investment	Usually no external equity, some business angel involvement possible
	Financing mix	High amount of external equity, some debt financing, intensive use of subsidies	Mix of external capital, soft loans, and subsidies	Internal funding, debt, and some soft loans
Human resources	*Balanced team*	Surrogate entrepreneur or hired guns	Technical scientists act as entrepreneurs	Technical scientists
	Sectoral experience	Management experience, research excellence	Few with experience	Considerable sector experience
Social resources	*Partnership at start-up*	Formal partnerships with stakeholders (venture capital, technology providers)	None	Formal availability of lead user

Source: Wright et al. (2007)

new growth firms and markets. These spin-offs typically have a patent-protected prototype that can be sold to generate revenue. They are able to attract external funding from public or PE funds linked to the university or public research lab. Often, they begin with a business model that essentially follows a contract research or consulting path and attempts to identify a product to commercialize. In the early phases of the start-up, the business model may not be clear and there can be a need to adapt it significantly as the venture emerges.

Lifestyle type spin-offs generally start small typically without formal IP from the university, but may build on consultancy activities of an academic with expertise in a particular area. Even if they remain as low-growth-oriented firms, their value added as a population might be economically significant since large numbers of this type of spin-off tend to be created. Technology transfer officers in universities usually tend to show very little support for these spin-offs as the upside possibilities are limited. Yet they are less demanding in terms of human, financial, and technological resources, and they can increase the visibility of the university in the host region. This type of spin-off forms the heart of the entrepreneurial university.

Entrepreneurial ventures are rarely created fully formed. They generally evolve through various phases over time. This evolution can be especially challenging for academic spin-off firms aiming to develop innovations where neither the initial product nor the potential market is evident at the outset. To be able to evolve successfully, academic spin-offs need to address the following four specific critical junctures:

- *Opportunity recognition*: Requires the spin-off to acquire the capability to synthesize scientific knowledge with an understanding of the market to which it might apply. There may be a need for networks of market contacts outside the scientific environment of the university.

- *Entrepreneurial commitment*: Requires the spin-off to acquire an entrepreneurial champion, whether the academic or a surrogate entrepreneur, committed to the development of the venture. Where this is a problem, it appears to arise from universities not providing sufficient resources and network contacts, or not developing appropriate incentives and policies.

- *Credibility*: Requires the spin-off to address the liabilities of newness and smallness. Credibility with trading partners and financiers is particularly problematical here because of the lack of commercial track record of the academic entrepreneurs, the often intangible nature of the spin-off firm's resources at this early stage, and the non-commercial environment from which the spin-off is emerging. Building links with surrogate entrepreneurs during earlier development phases, together with demonstrating proof of concept and the potential for a portfolio of products, and relocation in commercial premises away from the university can help signal a commercial approach to prospective customers and investors.

- *Sustainable returns*: Require the spin-off to develop entrepreneurial capabilities that enable it to reconfigure deficiencies from earlier phases into resource strengths, capabilities, and social capital.

Academic spin-offs adopt different types of growth strategy to exploit the opportunities generated by the IP emanating from laboratories. A product market strategy is more likely to aim at achieving growth in terms of revenues to create a sustainable growing business. Conversely, a financial market strategy places greater emphasis on creating value to enable the business to list on a stock market, or be sold to a strategic partner. Growing value can be achieved through building up the value of the science and technology in the business, even if no product sales are generated, or through a hybrid strategy of both building the value of the technology and generating sales, perhaps initially from consulting and services. The nature of the venture's sector and appropriability regime, that is the ability to protect IP through patenting or copyright, which may differ greatly between, for example, biotech and information technology sectors, can influence this choice. The choice between these commercialization strategies will be influenced by accessibility to the necessary complementary assets associated with each growth strategy. Product market strategies imply a need to acquire human capital with commercialization expertise. Financial market strategies imply a need to access complementary human capital assets that can help develop the technology.

Social enterprises

Social entrepreneurship involves the recognition of a social problem and the use of entrepreneurial principles to organize, create, and manage a social venture to achieve social, cultural, and or environmental change. In contrast to traditional commercial entrepreneurship, the underlying drive for a social entrepreneur is to generate positive returns to society, and to create difficult-to-measure social value (i.e. total wealth creation that can be financial and non-financial). Importantly, while social entrepreneurs are commonly associated with the voluntary and not-for-profit sectors, this need not preclude making a financial profit.

Although it has come to prominence in recent years, social entrepreneurship has a long history. The first social enterprise in England was established in the 1840s in Rochdale, Lancashire as a workers' cooperative to provide high-quality affordable food in response to factory conditions that were considered to be exploitative. A resurgence of social enterprise in the UK started in the mid 1990s associated with mushrooming in the formation of cooperatives, community enterprises, enterprising charities, and other forms of social business (http://www.socialenterprise.org.uk/about/about-social-enterprise). Nonetheless, social enterprises are diverse in goals, membership, legal form, and size, ranging from large national and international businesses to small community-based enterprises. A potential danger with the recent popularity of social enterprises is that commercial enterprises will attempt to hijack the 'social brand' in presenting their goods and services.

A social enterprise should have a clear sense of its 'social mission' in terms of what difference it is trying to make, who it aims to help, and how it plans to do it. Generally, social enterprises generate their income by selling goods and services rather than through grants and donations. Indeed, increasing numbers of charities are moving away from traditional models of fundraising and becoming more like trading businesses in order to ensure their sustainability. Social enterprises generally have clear rules that profits will be reinvested to further their social mission. Adopting charitable status, however, can offer tax breaks that help retain surpluses to further the social mission. While social enterprises can also use similar legal forms to standard companies and cooperatives, the community-interest company provides a legal form created specifically for social enterprises. It has a social objective that is regulated, ensuring that the organization cannot deviate from its social mission and that its assets are protected from being sold privately.

Social entrepreneurs vary in their entrepreneurial actions. Some social entrepreneurs are social bricoleurs who focus on addressing small-scale local social needs with whatever resources are to hand. A second group is social constructionists who develop goods and services to meet needs not adequately addressed by existing institutions and businesses; their activities can range from small to large scale. A third group is social engineers who identify systemic problems and address them through radical changes built upon harnessing popular political support. The social value created by these different types of social entrepreneurs may vary because of the different contexts in which they operate and their different 'political' goals.

A social enterprise's primary purpose is its social and/or environmental mission. Notably, a social enterprise tries to maximize the amount of social good it creates balanced against its financial goals. However, an ethical business attempts to minimize its negative impact on society or the environment.

In the United States, the social entrepreneurship phenomenon is mainstream, with *Forbes* magazine publishing a list of the top social entrepreneurs as well as its traditional 'rich list'. Social enterprises are engaged in a diverse range of sectors with a variety of social objectives. Notable social entrepreneur examples are: Jordan Kassalow, an optometrist by training, who runs an organization that sells ready-made reading glasses to people in the developing world; Sam Goldman and Ned Tozun of D.Light Design, who manufacture inexpensive lamps and sell them in communities that do not have reliable electricity; Tom Skazy, who dropped out of Princeton to create Terracycle, which sells fertilizer and over 250 products made from sixty waste streams; and Jane Chen, who established a company to manufacture a sleeping bag-like device called the 'Thermpod', which warms low-birthweight babies in hospitals and clinics that have unreliable electricity and heat lamps.

Businessweek's readers' top nominated for-profit social enterprise in 2012 was The Paradigm Project, which sells clean-burning wood or charcoal cookstoves in Kenya and Guatemala. United Nations-sanctioned auditors document how much emissions the stoves save, and Paradigm sells the carbon offsets the auditors award it. Another example, Sseko Designs, helps disadvantaged women in Uganda with academic promise to earn money to pay for university. The US-based business teaches participants how to sew. After working for nine months at its factory in the capital city of Kampala, participants leave with enough money to attend the first year of school.

In the UK, *The Big Issue*, the Eden Project, and Jamie Oliver's restaurant Fifteen are examples of social enterprises. Also in the UK, Cafédirect is the UK's largest fair trade hot drinks company; the Elvis and Kresse Organization (EaKo) takes industrial waste materials, turns them into stylish luggage and handbags, and donates 50 per cent of the profits to the Fire Fighters Charity; Hill Holt Wood educates at-risk youths in the setting of an ancient woodland; Central Surrey Health is a pioneering social enterprise in the health-care world run by the nursing and therapy teams it employs; and Green-Works takes office furniture that would have been sent to landfill and offers it at a large discount to charities and other organizations. In addition, award-winners such as Divine Chocolate, a fair trade chocolate company co-owned by the cocoa farmers' cooperative KuapaKokoo in Ghana and Women like Us, which connects women with flexible employment, are social enterprises.

The Eco-Lighthouse Foundation promotes social enterprise and the Norwegian Ministry of the Environment supports this environmental certification programme. The foundation helps firms to conduct profitable and environmentally friendly operations. Practices that are environmentally friendly in their use of resources, energy, chemicals, waste disposal, transportation, and dealings with suppliers are promoted. Firms that obtain Eco-Lighthouse certification (ELC) can thus mobilize an observable high-quality legitimacy resource, which can be signalled to obtain resources from potential external resource providers. During the certification implementation process, each firm gains access to an external consultant. This consultant facilitates participating firms to develop strategies that comply with industry-specific requirements, but at the same time promotes sustained competitive advantage and financial viability. An independent third-party auditor ensures that only firms that implement all specified foundation practices (i.e. firm objectives, planning, quality control measurements, record keeping, and the training and education of employees) are awarded ELC. The ELC licence is valid for three years. It can be renewed if the firm complies with ELC requirements, which are continuously evaluated and increased relating to market and regulatory standards.

Chapter 7
The future

At the outset, we suggested that entrepreneurship was experiencing a golden age. If the golden age of entrepreneurship is to have a lasting impact on society several puzzles and challenges need to be addressed. Notably we need to consider that entrepreneurship has costs and shortcomings as well as benefits. These issues that need to be considered in the future are discussed in the following sections.

Firm growth

An important issue in entrepreneurship is whether it stops with the creation of a firm or whether it continues beyond this point. Our earlier chapters showed that entrepreneurship is a process that takes place over time and can continue in established firms. Some people also have careers in entrepreneurship, owning multiple firms over time. For entrepreneurship to make a contribution to society, it is important to go beyond a focus on the creation of firms, many of which close quite quickly after formation as highlighted in Chapter 5. Rather, greater impact involves addressing questions of how exploitation of an opportunity leads to growing and sustainable businesses.

While the effectuation and bricolage approaches provide exciting new directions into how entrepreneurs can create new firms in highly constrained resource contexts, they currently provide limited insights surrounding how new firms make the transition to high growth, the outcome currently being sought by governments throughout the world concerned with promoting economic development.

The results of a vast amount of research investigating the reasons surrounding how firms grow and why some new firms grow more than others have identified the importance of entrepreneur characteristics, availability of resources, the strategy adopted for the firm, industry context, and organizational structures and systems. The majority of attention has been on firm growth in employment or sales revenue. However, more limited attention has been directed towards firm profitability and survival, as well as broader measures of firm value including social value (i.e. total wealth creation, which can be financial and non-financial), as illustrated by social firms in Chapter 6. Also, the issue of entrepreneur rather than firm performance has attracted scant attention.

We highlight two particular unresolved puzzles. Resolution of these puzzles would contribute to increasing the societal contribution of entrepreneurship. This challenge is especially pertinent given that at the time of writing (spring 2013), governments worldwide face the challenge of developing policies to promote growth in an environment with severe financial constraints and double-dip recession.

The first puzzle concerns why there appears to be little correlation between growth in sales and growth in revenues in entrepreneurial firms. These two performance measures are not alternative measures of the same thing, and the lack of correlation provides a clue that different entrepreneurial processes underpin firm growth. For example, while we might typically think of growth in terms of selling products to final consumers in a product market, this is a narrow view. Particularly in high-tech markets, entrepreneurs starting a firm may sell their technology to other large firms in an industry, for example through licensing. These incumbent firms can have the complementary resources to develop the technology into final products that would be beyond the start-up entrepreneur. Entrepreneurial start-ups in high-tech sectors may also focus on building the value of their technology, as illustrated in Chapter 3 with Renovo. Here entrepreneurs can create value by selling their business to an incumbent, or floating it on the stock market even though some firms might not have generated revenue from selling products to final customers. Rather than developing production and marketing capacity and being able to generate sales revenue quite soon after start-up, these firms face the challenges of obtaining funding rounds to bridge the so-called 'valley of death'. This is the gap between using or 'burning' initial funding and generating further funding from either sales revenue or a second round of external finance. In addition, firms may need to develop internationalization strategies because their markets are global ones. Here firms need to identify alliance partners and acquisition candidates, and build relationships with incumbent firms that could eventually acquire them.

The second puzzle is why patterns of growth are so varied. Relatively few entrepreneurial firms display strong, sustained growth. Some firms grow quickly at first and then fade. Other firms face difficulties but recover to become successful businesses. One explanation is that entrepreneurs differ in their abilities to discover, create, evaluate, and exploit opportunities with sustained growth potential. Entrepreneurs also differ with regard to their motivations toward firm growth. However, we still do not know why some entrepreneurs are more motivated than others to grow their firms, or are motivated to grow their firms in different ways. As illustrated in Chapter 5, we now know more about entrepreneurial cognition, but we still need to unpack the 'black box' of entrepreneurial cognitive processes by exploring how entrepreneurs *really* make the decisions to grow or not to grow firms. Because entrepreneurs have to repeatedly make sense of ambiguous and changing information in an uncertain external environment, people with a more intuitive and non-linear decision-making style may be better able to realize growth opportunities.

Contexts

In Chapter 4, we discussed how the social, geographical, and institutional context might influence whether someone becomes an entrepreneur. But contextual dimensions extend beyond geographical or spatial location within a particular country, industry, or market environment. Whether someone becomes an entrepreneur and whether they subsequently grow their business(es) also need to be understood in relation to the temporal dimension. At the firm level, this dimension relates to the particular phases of a firm's life cycle—that is, whether the sector is emerging, growing, in maturity, or in decline. In addition, the temporal dimension involves the individual entrepreneur level in terms of the stage of their entrepreneurial career. As illustrated in Chapter 4, entrepreneurial careers may take place within a single firm or in multiple ventures held sequentially or concurrently as a portfolio. The temporal dimension, also relates to national context. For example, some emerging and developed economies may have less urgency about the timely need to exploit opportunities. The cognitive processes and resource configuration behaviour of entrepreneurs in countries with a more urgent view of time may differ from those countries, typically underdeveloped ones, with a more lax perspective, where, for example, being well organized, getting to work on time, and delivering on time are more variable. These differences might have potentially major implications for the ability of entrepreneurship to contribute to societal wealth creation. Rather than focusing upon the firm there is a need to consider the entrepreneur as the unit of analysis in understanding the phases in the entrepreneurial process.

Promotion of entrepreneurship plays an important role in the development of national-level innovation. Traditionally, national innovation systems focus on the establishment of institutions that create and disseminate new knowledge through long-term research and development programmes, while entrepreneurship is often ignored. In fast-moving technology sectors, such approaches may be insufficient. William Baumol has argued that entrepreneurial innovation is the true source of national competitive advantage, and the challenge is to create an enabling context where entrepreneurial innovation can flourish. Such an environment may involve defining, creating, and supporting an entrepreneurial ecosystem involving relations between entrepreneurs and their firms, universities, potential and actual industrial partners, trading partners, finance providers, and government support. This represents a radical departure from traditional national innovation systems and industrial clusters. So, rather than focusing upon entrepreneurial firms in isolation, there is a need to focus on the role of the entrepreneurial ecosystem as a whole, and the processes of how it is developed, nurtured, adapted, and sustained.

Spread and transformation

Entrepreneurship has a wider application than just the start-up of a new firm. Notably, as illustrated in Chapter 6, it can involve a range of different modes. For example, it relates to CE, social enterprise, entrepreneurship in family firms, and the entrepreneurship that can be released through the change in ownership resulting from a management buyout.

Post the 2008 financial crisis, we appear to be witnessing a major re-evaluation of the goals of entrepreneurship. Rather than thinking in terms of purely private financial gains, the emergence of social entrepreneurs represents a new development, which plays a role in filling gaps in provision by official agencies in an era of tight budgetary constraints.

Interestingly, many MBA students in business schools are now writing business plans for social rather than for purely commercial enterprises.

Entrepreneurship plays a vital role in the rehabilitation of servicemen and war veterans who joined the armed forces post 9/11 in 2001, especially those whose injuries make it virtually impossible for them to either find or hold down a regular job. A notable example of how this is being facilitated is the Barnes Family Entrepreneurship Bootcamp for Veterans with Disabilities programme started at Syracuse University in 2007 in the United States. This initiative has now been adopted by other universities throughout the United States such as Mays Business School at Texas A&M University. The programme provides cutting-edge training in the skills necessary to successfully launch and grow a new business through online coursework, an intense residency experience, and twelve months of support and mentorship to veterans with service-connected disabilities at no cost to participants.

Address extreme poverty

According to the World Bank, an estimated 1.5 billion people live in extreme poverty, subsisting on an average of US $1.25 or less per day. While international and national governmental agencies have for many decades contributed to the alleviation of those living in such poverty, it is increasingly recognized that this top-down approach on its own is insufficient. In line with the saying 'give someone a fish and they eat for a day, teach them to fish and they can feed themselves for life', we are seeing a surge in attempts to promote entrepreneurship at the local level in underdeveloped countries.

Some schemes are promoted within particular countries and funded by national governments. For example, the Kenya Entrepreneurship Empowerment Foundation (KEEF) is a non-profit-making non-governmental organization devoted to poverty eradication among marginalized groups in Kenya, focusing primarily on women and young people. The foundation provides micro credit at low rates of interest and support for the establishment of sustainable micro enterprise in Kenya (http://www.mixmarket.org/mfi/keef#ixzz29f1eIW2K). Other schemes are funded by private foundations.

Nevertheless, such poverty represents major challenges for entrepreneurship. Throughout this book, we have suggested that context matters and that the entrepreneurial process is interlinked with context. In many underdeveloped countries, weak or absent supporting institutions frustrate the ability of people in poverty to become entrepreneurs. For example, the Challenging the Frontiers of Poverty Reduction (CFPR) programme of the BRAC non-governmental office in Bangladesh aimed to overcome the problem that traditional microfinance programmes were not reaching the poorest of the poor. The interplay between the existing power structure, legacy institutions, and recently introduced institutional practices regarding microfinance created a gap in the institutional context. BRAC was able to fill this gap by drawing upon its own internal experiences and networks built over many years working in rural areas of Bangladesh, and upon lessons from the external institutional context by engaging with existing customary practices of support to the poor, religious beliefs, and popular theatre performances.

Valuable though these developments undoubtedly are, their ability to create high-growth firms generating significant local employment and wealth may be limited. The emergence of such enterprises may need to await the emergence of stronger institutional frameworks and factor markets. These can facilitate key developments such as the establishment of major financial institutions, the rule of law and the enforcement of contracts, as well as the development of infrastructures that facilitate mobility of resources and the distribution of goods and services. The extent to which emerging economies are developing their institutions and factor markets is highly varied. A growing number of countries are becoming 'mid-range economies', which display to various degrees the characteristics of developed market economies. Poland has experienced significant institutional development since the fall of the Berlin Wall, and has joined the European Union. India has relatively strong democratic political institutions, although its infrastructure development remains relatively poor. Thailand has undertaken major infrastructure projects but political instability has been a concern. Entrepreneurial firms from these countries are becoming increasingly well placed to compete in world markets, but they still need home country government support for their internationalization activities. Rather than competing only on the basis of low cost, some of these firms now have the potential to penetrate developed markets on the basis of their advanced high-tech products.

New forms of finance

As new forms of entrepreneurship emerge, they will challenge traditional notions of the gap between the financial needs of entrepreneurial firms and the available sources of finance. Revolutionary developments in technology are especially having important impacts. New technology and media firms are challenging and even superseding the traditional role of seed VC. For example, mobile technologies, social networking tools, and crowdfunding mechanisms make it easier to pool and distribute small amounts of seed capital, or microfinance, from individuals who want to invest in or lend to entrepreneurial ventures. Accelerators and start-up factories, such as Seedcamp, can also play an important role in enabling entrepreneurs to overcome the initial phases of start-up. Notably, they can provide small amounts of pre-seed finance in return for equity as well as initial business development support.

Microfinance is increasingly playing a central role in stimulating and nurturing entrepreneurial activity in developing countries. Here microfinance provides entrepreneurs with small amounts of finance that may be impossible to find elsewhere in contexts associated with undeveloped capital markets and an absence of personal wealth.

While microfinance has emerged as uncollateralized start-up loans for people living in poverty, it is developing into a variety of debt- and equity-based financing possibilities. Sources of this microfinance are proliferating and include banks, savings and loan organizations, for-profit investment funds, insurance companies, mobile network operators, as well as individuals acting as microangels and microlenders. Migrant workers from developing countries remitting some of their earnings to family members back home are a growing source of finance. Some of these sources are for-profit businesses, while others are charities and not-for-profit organizations.

Currently, we need to know more about which of the emerging forms of microfinance are most suitable and effective in specific contexts. The most influential forms of microfinance in promoting innovative high-tech entrepreneurs in developed economies may not be the same as those supporting entrepreneurs to get out of desperate poverty in undeveloped economies.

We have little evidence relating to the longer-term performance of entrepreneurs funded with microfinance. Microfinance may facilitate business initiation but it may be more limited in helping these firms to grow and to employ other local people who can be taken out of poverty. The challenge then is to develop mechanisms that can help bridge the development of these microfinance firms from start-ups to sustainable growing firms. As we know from studies of VC support for entrepreneurs, besides finance it is also necessary to provide other support to entrepreneurs in the form of skills and social capital to grow a business successfully.

Dark side of entrepreneurship

Besides these exciting and novel positive developments generated by entrepreneurship, the negative aspects are sometimes forgotten, or neglected. The issue of high new firm closure rates was raised in Chapter 1 with practitioners assuming 'productive churn'. Although we may be witnessing a golden age of entrepreneurship worldwide in terms of policy and research, there is a dark side that has yet to be fully acknowledged. Two particular aspects of this dark side stand out.

First, William Baumol highlighted that a dark side, or destructive aspect, of entrepreneurship could arise from shortcomings in the institutional rules of the game that allowed and even rewarded corruption and illegal entrepreneurship. Some entrepreneurs may use their wealth to bribe politicians who will protect their interests. In Chapter 1, we highlighted that entrepreneurs can provide competition for existing firms. However, they can have an adverse effect by using their wealth to stifle entry of new innovative firms. Also, they can thus avert competition and delay technological progress and benefits to society.

Some entrepreneurial activities constitute the informal economy, which can bring both costs and benefits to society. Informal economy activities include unregistered businesses that avoid corporate taxes and violate labour regulations, and those businesses that sell counterfeit products. Estimates suggest that informal activities account for between 10 and 20 per cent of GDP in mature economies, and up to 60 per cent in emerging economies. Informal entrepreneurial activities may be illegal, but they arise where formal legal institutions are deemed by a significant group in society to be too restrictive or corrupt to be legitimate. Informal entrepreneurs can compete unfairly with formal businesses, but in some cases may enable formal businesses to operate effectively.

Rapid industrialization confined to some parts of a country may lead to migration to urban areas. This can result in many individuals having to operate in the informal economy in order to subsist. Necessity drives some people to become informal entrepreneurs. This is because entrepreneurship is the only source of income for those unable to gain formal employment. Such entrepreneurs often face major barriers to obtaining resources for entrepreneurship, and may use resources discarded by others (engaging in bricolage as highlighted in Chapter 2) as inputs into their activities (in many countries, for example India, waste such as old tyres can be used as a fuel or recyclable goods can be recovered from waste tips and sold).

Excessive bureaucracy in both developed and emerging economies can generate significant costs and hurdles that stifle formal entrepreneurship. In Chapter 1, we noted that there are marked differences between countries in the ease of starting businesses.

A second aspect of the dark side of entrepreneurship concerns the personal impact. In contrast to the private benefits of amassing significant wealth from entrepreneurship, the costs to family and personal health are often neglected. The downside to the entrepreneur's qualities of tenacity and willingness to work long hours can be a negative impact upon personal relationships. Some entrepreneurs may not be around enough to sustain relationships, which can lead to divorce from partners and estrangement from children. Also, the single-minded belief in what is needed to make a firm work can create conflicts and unwillingness to cooperate with family members. These tensions may be exacerbated where family members are involved in the entrepreneurial firm.

Failure of entrepreneurial firms may amplify these effects on personal and family life. The loss of homes that have been used as collateral for business loans when a firm fails can be especially challenging to personal relationships. We saw in Chapter 5 how the loss of a firm that the entrepreneur was closely involved with can generate feelings of grief and depression. These entrepreneurs may cease to be entrepreneurs, never to return if they are unable to move on. Their children could also be discouraged from becoming entrepreneurs—like Dean Shepherd and one of the authors of this volume, who both became professors of entrepreneurship instead!

The little evidence we do have on how being an entrepreneur takes its toll shows that entrepreneurs report higher levels of social isolation compared to senior managers. Some entrepreneurs experience insecurity not only about their jobs but also about the future. Further, some entrepreneurs report high incidence of conflicts, accidents, illnesses, stress levels, fatigue and exhaustion, and burnout.

Where do we go from here?

Expectations about the ability of entrepreneurs to deliver economic benefits are high, and have perhaps become too high. While some entrepreneurial firms can create significant private and social benefits, firm failure rates are high, and firm growth presents major challenges. There are significant downsides as well as upsides generated by entrepreneurship. There is a need for greater recognition of these two sides to entrepreneurship among policymakers and educators. Educational programmes need to go beyond proselytizing to alerting potential entrepreneurs to the dangers and pitfalls. This is not to undermine the importance of entrepreneurship, but rather to help build a sustainable entrepreneurial culture rather than one that collapses amid disillusionment.

Further reading

Chapter 1: The importance of entrepreneurship

Acs, Z. J. (1996). *Small Firms and Economic Growth. The International Library of Critical Writings in Economics 61*. Cheltenham: Edward Elgar.

Bosma, N. and Harding, R. (2007). *GEM 2006 Results*. London and Boston, MA: Babson College and London Business School.

Bower, T. (2008). *Branson*. London: Harper Perennial.

Branson, R. (2011). *Business Stripped Bare: Adventures of a Global Entrepreneur*. London: Penguin Group.

Bridge, S., O'Neill, K., and Martin, F. (2009). *Understanding Enterprise, Entrepreneurship & Small Business*, 3rd edition. Basingstoke: Palgrave Macmillan.

Bygrave, B. (2004). The entrepreneurial process. In W. Bygrave and A. E. Zacharkis (eds) *The Portable MBA in Entrepreneurship*. Hoboken, NJ: John Wiley & Sons, pp. 1–28.

Bygrave, W. (2006). The entrepreneurship paradigm (I) revisited. In H. Neergard and J. Parm Ulhoi (eds) *Handbook of Qualitative Research Methods in Entrepreneurship*. Cheltenham, UK: Edward Elgar Publishing, Inc., pp. 17–48.

Cunningham, J. B. and Lischeron, J. (1991). Defining Entrepreneurship. *Journal of Small Business Management*, 29 (1): 45–61.

Department of Trade and Industry. (2004). *A Government Action Plan for Small Business. Making the UK the Best Place in the World to Start and Grow a Business: The Evidence Base*. London: DTI, Small Business Service.

Drakopoulou Dodd, S. and Anderson, A. R. (2007). Mumpsimus and the Mything of the Individualistic Entrepreneur. *International Small Business Journal*, 25 (4): 341–360.

Gartner, W. B. (1985). A Conceptual Framework for Describing the Phenomenon of New Venture Creation. *Academy of Management Review*, 10 (4): 696–706.

Hannan, M. T. and Caroll, G. R. (2000). *The Demography of Corporations and Industries*. Princeton, NJ: Princeton University Press.

Hébert, R. and Link, A. A. (2006). Historical Perspectives on the Entrepreneur. *Foundations and Trends® in Entrepreneurship*, 2 (4): 261–408.

Kelley, D., Singer, S., and Herrington, M. (2012). *2011 Global Report*. Global Entrepreneurship Research Association (GERA). Wellesley: Babson College.

Kets de Vries, M. (1997). Creative rebels with a cause. In S. Birley and D. F. Muzyka (eds) *Mastering Enterprise*. London: Pitman Publishing, pp. 6–9.

Landström, H. (2005). *Pioneers in Entrepreneurship and Small Business Research*. New York: Springer.

Low, M. B. and MacMillan, I. C. (1988). Entrepreneurship: Past Research and Future Challenges. *Journal of Management*, 14 (2): 139–161.

Moroz, P. and Hindle, K. (2012). Entrepreneurship as a process: toward harmonizing multiple perspectives. *Entrepreneurship Theory and Practice*, 36 (4): 781–818.

Organisation for Economic Co-Operation and Development (OECD). (1998). *Fostering Entrepreneurship*. Paris: Organisation for Economic Co-Operation and Development.

Reynolds, P., Storey, D. J., and Westhead, P. (1994). Cross-National Comparisons of the Variation in New Firm Formation Rates. *Regional Studies*, 28 (4): 443–456.

Reynolds, P. R., Camp, S. M., Bygrave, W. D., Autio, E., and Hay, M. (2001). *Global Entrepreneurship Monitor: 2001 Executive Report*. Kansas City, MO: Kauffman Center for Entrepreneurial Leadership at the Ewing Marion Kauffman Foundation.

Schumpeter, J. A. (1934). *The Theory of Economic Development*. Cambridge, MA: Harvard University Press.

Stinchcombe, A. L. (1965). Social Structure and Organizations. In J. G. March (ed.) *Handbook of Organizations*. Chicago: Rand McNally, pp. 142–193.

Storey, D. J. (1994). *Understanding the Small Business Sector*.
London, Thomson Learning.

Storey, D., Keasey, K., Watson, R., and Wynarczyk, P. (1987). *The
Performance of Small Firms: Profits, Jobs and Failures*. London:
Croom Helm.

Ucbasaran, D., Westhead, P., and Wright, M. (2001). The Focus of
Entrepreneurial Research: Contextual and Process Issues.
Entrepreneurship Theory and Practice, 25 (4): 57–80.

Westhead, P., Ucbasaran, D., and Wright, M. (2004). Policy Toward
Novice, Serial and Portfolio Entrepreneurs. *Environment and
Planning C: Government and Policy*, 22 (6): 779–798.

Westhead, P., Wright, M., and McElwee, G. (2011). *Entrepreneurship:
Perspectives and Cases*. Harlow: Pearson Education Limited.

Zahra, S. A. (2007). Contextualizing Theory Building in Entrepreneurship
Research. *Journal of Business Venturing*, 22 (3): 443–452.

Chapter 2: Discovering and creating opportunities

Alvarez, S. A. and Barney, J. B. (2007). Discovery and Creation:
Alternative Theories of Entrepreneurial Action. *Strategic
Entrepreneurship Journal*, 1 (1–2): 11–26.

Baker, T. and Nelson, R. E. (2005). Creating Something from Nothing:
Resource Construction through Entrepreneurial Bricolage.
Adminsistrative Science Quarterly, 50 (3): 329–366.

Barney, J. B. (1991). Firm Resources and Sustained Competitive
Advantage. *Journal of Management*, 17 (1): 99–120.

Cantillon, R. (1755). *Essai sur la Nature du Commerce en General*.
Translated by H. Higgs (1931). London: Macmillan.

Casson, M. (1982). *The Entrepreneur: An Economic Theory*. Oxford:
Martin Robertson.

Cuevas, J. G. (1994). Towards a Taxonomy of Entrepreneurial
Theories. *International Small Business Journal*, 12 (4): 77–88.

Di Domenico, M. L., Haugh, H., and Tracey, P. (2010). Social
Bricolage: Theorizing Social Value Creation in Social Enterprises.
Entrepreneurship Theory and Practice, 34 (4): 681–703.

Fiet, J. O. (2002). *The Systematic Search for Entrepreneurial
Discoveries*. London: Quorum Books.

Hannan, M. T. and Carroll, G. R. (1992). *Dynamics of Organizational
Populations: Density, Legitimation and Competition*. New York:
Oxford University Press.

Harmeling, S. (2011). Contingency as an Entrepreneurial Resource: How Private Obsession Fulfils Public Needs. *Journal of Business Venturing*, 26 (3): 293–305.

Kirzner, I. M. (1973). *Competition and Entrepreneurship*. Chicago: University of Chicago Press.

Knight, F. H. (1921). *Risk, Uncertainty and Profit* (ed. G. J. Stigler). Chicago: University of Chicago.

Phillips, N. and Tracey, P. (2007). Opportunity Recognition, Entrepreneurial Capabilities and Bricolage: Connecting Institutional Theory and Entrepreneurship in Strategic Organization. *Strategic Organization*, 5 (3): 313–320.

Read, S., Sarasvathy, S., Dew, N., Wiltbank, R., and Ohlsson, A. (2011). *Effectual Entrepreneurship*. Abingdon, New York: Routledge.

Sarasvathy, S. (2008). *Effectuation: Elements of Entrepreneurial Expertise*. Cheltenham, UK: Edward Elgar.

Say, J. B. (1803). *A Treatise on Political Economy: Or, the Production, Distribution and Consumption of Wealth*. New York: Augustus M. Kelley (reprinted 1964).

Schumpeter, J. A. (1934). *The Theory of Economic Development*. Cambridge, MA: Harvard University Press.

Shackle, G. (1979). *Imagination and the Nature of Choice*. Edinburgh: Edinburgh University Press.

Shane, S. and Venkataraman, S. (2000). The Promise of Entrepreneurship as a Field of Research. *Academy of Management Review*, 25 (1): 217–226.

Solesvik, M. and Westhead, P. (2012). Female and Male Opportunity Effectuation and Bricolage in a Resource-Constrained Environment. Durham: Durham University Business School, working paper.

Westhead, P., Ucbasaran, D., Wright, M., and Martin, F. (2003). *Habitual Entrepreneurs in Scotland, Characteristics, Search Processes, Learning and Performance—Summary Report*. Glasgow: Scottish Enterprise.

Chapter 3: Exploiting opportunities

Barney, J. B. (1991). Firm Resources and Sustained Competitive Advantage. *Journal of Management*, 17 (1): 99–120.

Barney, J. B. (2001). Is the Resource-Based 'View' a Useful Perspective for Strategic Management Research? Yes. *Academy of Management Review*, 26 (1): 41–56.

Brinckmann, J., Grichnik, D., and Kapsa, D. (2010). Should Entrepreneurs Plan or Just Storm the Castle? A Meta-Analysis on Contextual Factors Impacting the Business Planning-Performance Relationship in Small Firms. *Journal of Business Venturing*, 25 (1): 24–40.

Eisenhardt, K. M. and Martin, J. A. (2000). Dynamic Capabilities: What Are They? *Strategic Management Journal*, 21 (10–11): 1105–1121.

George, G. and Bock, A. J. (2012). *Models of Opportunity: How Entrepreneurs Design Firms to Achieve the Unexpected*. Cambridge: Cambridge University Press.

Hitt, M. A., Ireland, R. D., Sirmon, D. G., and Trahms, C. A. (2011). Strategic Entrepreneurship: Creating Value for Individuals, Organizations, and Society. *Academy of Management Perspectives* 25 (2): 57–75.

Marshall, A. (1890). *Principles of Economics* (ed. G. W. Guilleband). 2 volumes, 9th edition. London: Macmillan (1961).

Marshall, A. (1920). *Principles of Economics*. 8th edition, reset 1949. London: Macmillan.

McWatt, J. (2010). Welsh-Based Company Coffee#1 Beats Big Boys to Award. *The Western Mail*, 6th March, 2010.

Penrose, E. (1959). *The Theory of the Growth of the Firm*. Oxford: Blackwell Scientific Publications.

Pfeffer, J. and Salancik, G. R. (1978). *The External Control of Organizations: A Resource Dependence Perspective*. New York: Harper & Row.

Rasmussen, E., Mosey, S., and Wright, M. (2011). The Evolution of Entrepreneurial Competencies: A Longitudinal Study of University Spin-off Venture Emergence. *Journal of Management Studies*, 48 (6): 1314–1345.

Sirmon, D., Hitt, M. A., Ireland, R. D., and Gilbert, B. A. (2011). Resource Orchestration to Create Competitive Advantage: Breadth, Depth and Life Cycle Effects. *Journal of Management*, 37 (5): 1390–1412.

Villaneuva J., Van de Ven, A. H., and Sapienza, H. J. (2012). Resource Mobilization in Entrepreneurial Firms. *Journal of Business Venturing*, 27 (1): 19–30.

Wright, M., Clarysse, B., and Mosey, S. (2012). Strategic Entrepreneurship, Resource Orchestration and Growing Spin-offs from Universities. *Technology Analysis and Strategic Management*, 24: 911–927.

Anna, A. L., Chandler, G. N., Jansen, E., and Mero, N. P. (2000). Women Business Owners in Traditional and Non-Traditional Industries. *Journal of Business Venturing*, 15 (3): 279–303.

Becker, G. S. (1975). *Human Capital*. New York: National Bureau of Economic Research.

Birley, S. and Westhead, P. (1994). A Taxonomy of Business Start-Up Reasons and their Impact on Firm Growth and Size. *Journal of Business Venturing*, 9 (1): 7–31.

Carter, S., Anderson, S., and Shaw, E. (2001). *Women's Business Ownership: A Review of the Academic, Popular and Internet Literature*. Sheffield: Small Business Service, Research Report: RR002/01.

Department of Trade and Industry (2004). *A Government Action Plan for Small Business. Making the UK the Best Place in the World to Start and Grow a Business: The Evidence Base*. London: DTI, Small Business Service.

Gartner, W. B. (1989). 'Who is an Entrepreneur?' Is the Wrong Question. *Entrepreneurship Theory and Practice*, 13 (4): 47–68.

Gibb, A. A. (1987). Enterprise Culture—Its Meaning and Implications for Education and Training. *Journal of European Industrial Training*, 11 (2): 2–38.

Gibb, A. and Ritchie, J. (1982). Understanding the Process of Starting Small Businesses. *European Small Business Journal*, 1 (1): 26–45.

Gimeno, J., Folta, T. B., Cooper, A. C., and Woo, C. Y. (1997). Survival of the Fittest? Entrepreneurial Human Capital and the Persistence of Underperforming Firms. *Administrative Science Quarterly*, 42 (4): 750–783.

Goffee, R. and Scase, R. (1987). Patterns of Business Proprietorship among Women in Britain. In R. Goffee and R. Scase (eds) *Entrepreneurship in Europe*. London: Croom Helm, pp. 60–82.

Holmquist, C. and Sundin, E. (1990). What's Special About Highly Educated Women Entrepreneurs. *Entrepreneurship and Regional Development*, 2 (2): 181–193.

Gupta, V. K., Turban, D. B., Wasti, A. A., and Sikdar, A. (2009). The Role of Gender Streotypes in Perceptions of Entrepreneurs and Intentions to Become an Entrepreneur. *Entrepreneurship Theory and Practice*, 33 (2): 397–417.

Kariv, D. (2013). *Female Entrepreneurship and the New Venture Creation: An International Perspective*. London: Routledge.

Kelley, D., Singer, S. and Herrington, M. (2012). *2011 Global Report*. Global Entrepreneurship Research Association (GERA). Wellesley: Babson College.

Licht, A. N. and Siegel, J. I. (2006). The Social Dimensions of Entrepreneurship. In M. Casson, B. Yeung, A. Basu and N. Wadeson (eds) *The Oxford Handbook of Entrepreneurship*. Oxford: Oxford University Press, pp. 511–539.

MacMillan, I. C. (1986). To Really Learn About Entrepreneurship, Let's Study Habitual Entrepreneurs. *Journal of Business Venturing*, 1 (3): 241–243.

Miner, J. B. (2000). Testing a Psychological Typology of Entrepreneurship Using Business Founders. *Journal of Applied Behavioral Science*, 36 (1): 43–70.

Reynolds, P., Storey, D. J., and Westhead, P. (1994). Cross-National Comparisons of the Variation in New Firm Formation Rates. *Regional Studies*, 28 (4): 443–456.

Robb, A. M. and Watson, J. (2012). Gender Differences in Firm Performance: Evidence from New Ventures in the United States. *Journal of Business Venturing*, 27 (5): 279–303.

Schwab, K. (2011). *The Global Competitiveness Report 2011-12*. Geneva: World Economic Forum.

Smith, N. R. (1967). *The Entrepreneur and His Firm: The Relationship Between Type of Man and Type of Company*. East Lansing, Michigan: Michigan State University Press.

Ucbasaran, D., Alsos, G. A., Westhead, P., and Wright, M. (2008). Habitual Entrepreneurs. *Foundations and Trends® in Entrepreneurship*, 4 (4): 309–449.

Watson, J. (2002). Comparing the Performance of Male- and Female-Controlled Businesses: Relating Outputs to Inputs. *Entrepreneurship Theory and Practice*, 26 (3): 91–100.

Westhead, P., Ucbasaran, D., Wright, M., and Binks, M. (2005). Policy Toward Novice, Serial and Portfolio Entrepreneurs. *Small Business Economics*, 25 (2): 109–132.

Westhead, P. and Wright, M. (1998). Novice, Portfolio and Serial Founders: Are They Different? *Journal of Business Venturing*, 13 (3): 173–204.

Chapter 5: Entrepreneurial thinking and learning

Ajzen, I. (2002). Perceived Behavior Control, Self-Efficacy, Locus of Control, and the Theory of Planned Behavior. *Journal of Applied Social Psychology*, 32 (4): 665–683.

Bandura, A. (1995). Perceived Self-Efficacy. In A. S. R. Manstead and M. Hawstone (eds) *The Blackwell Encyclopaedia of Social Psychology*. Oxford: Blackwell Publishers Ltd, pp. 434–436.

Baron, R. A. (1998). Cognitive Mechanisms in Entrepreneurship: Why and When Entrepreneurs Think Differently Than Other People. *Journal of Business Venturing*, 13 (4): 275–294.

Baron, R. A. (2004). The Cognitive Perspective, A Valuable Tool for Answering Entrepreneurship's Basic 'Why' Questions. *Journal of Business Venturing*, 19 (2): 221–239.

Busenitz, L. W. and Barney, J. B. (1997). Differences Between Entrepreneurs and Managers in Large Organizations: Biases and Heuristics in Strategic Decision-Making. *Journal of Business Venturing*, 12 (1): 9–30.

Gartner, W. B. (1989). 'Who is an Entrepreneur?' is the Wrong Question. *Entrepreneurship Theory and Practice*, 13 (4): 47–68.

Gregoire, D. A., Corbett, A. C., and McMullen, J. S. (2011). The Cognitive Perspective in Entrepreneurship: An Agenda for Future Research. *Journal of Management Studies*, 48 (6): 1443–1477.

Kets de Vries, M. F. R. (1977). The Entrepreneurial Personality: A Person at the Crossroads. *Journal of Management Studies*, 14 (1): 34–57.

McClelland, D. C. (1961). *The Achieving Society*. New Jersey, Princeton: Van Nostrand.

McGrath, R. G. (1999). Falling Forward: Real Options Reasoning and Entrepreneurial Failure. *Academy of Management Review*, 24 (1): 13–30.

Miner, J. B., Smith, N. R., and Bracker, J. S. (1992). Predicting Firm Survival from a Knowledge of Entrepreneur Task Motivation. *Entrepreneurship and Regional Development*, 4 (2): 145–153.

Mitchell, R. K., Busenitz, L., Lant, T., McDougall, P. P., Morse, E. A., and Smith, B. (2002). Entrepreneurial Cognition Theory: Rethinking the People Side of Entrepreneurship Research. *Entrepreneurship Theory and Practice*, 27 (2): 93–104.

Rotter, J. (1966). Generalised Expectancies for Internal Versus External Control of Reinforcement. *Psychological Monographs*, 80 (1): 1–27.

Shepherd, D. (2003). Learning from Business Failure: Propositions about the Grief Recovery Process for the Self-employed. *Academy of Management Review*, 28 (2): 318–329.

Sitkin, S. B. (1992). Learning through failure: the strategy of small losses. In B. M. Staw and L. L. Cummings (eds) *Research in Organizational Behavior*. Greenwich, CT: JAI Press, pp. 231–266.

Tversky, A. and Kahneman, D. (1974). Judgement Under Uncertainty: Heuristics and Biases. *Science*, 185 (4157): 1124–1131.

Ucbasaran, D., Alsos, G. A., Westhead, P., and Wright, M. (2008). Habitual Entrepreneurs. *Foundations and Trends® in Entrepreneurship*, 4 (4): 309–449.

Ucbasaran, D., Westhead, P., Wright, M., and Flores, M. (2010). The Nature of Entrepreneurial Experience, Business Failure and Comparative Optimism. *Journal of Business Venturing*, 25 (6): 541–555.

Westhead, P., Robson, P., and Wright, M. (2012). *Entrepreneurial Learning, Repeat Entrepreneurs and Business Ownership Success and Failure Experience*. Durham: Durham University Business School working paper.

Zhao, H., Seibert, S. E., and Lumpkin, G. T. (2010). The Relationship of Personality to Entrepreneurial Intentions and Performance: A Meta-Analytic Review. *Journal of Management*, 36 (2): 381–404.

Chapter 6: Forms of entrepreneurial venture

Acs, Z. J., Audretsch, D. B., and Feldman, M. P. (1992). Real Effects of Academic Research: Comment. *American Economic Review*, 82: 363–367.

Austin, J., Stevenson, H., and Wei-Skillern, J. (2006). Social and Commercial Entrepreneurship: Same, Different or Both? *Entrepreneurship Theory and Practice*, 30 (1): 1–22.

Clarysse, B., Wright, M., Lockett, A., van de Elde, E., and Vohora, A. (2005). Spinning Out New Ventures: A Typology of Incubation Strategies from European Research Institutions. *Journal of Business Venturing*, 20 (2): 183–216.

Covin, J. and Miles, M. (1999). Corporate Entrepreneurship and the Pursuit of Competitive Advantage. *Entrepreneurship Theory and Practice*, 23 (3): 47–63.

Di Domenico, M. L., Haugh, H., and Tracey, P. (2010). Social Bricolage: Theorizing Social Value Creation in Social Enterprises. *Entrepreneurship Theory and Practice*, 34 (4): 681–703.

Franklin, S., Wright, M., and Lockett, A. (2001). Academic and Surrogate Entrepreneurs in University Spin-out Companies. *Journal of Technology Transfer*, 26 (1–2): 127–141.

Hoy, F. and Verser, T. G. (1994). Emerging Business, Emerging Field: Entrepreneurship and the Family Firm. *Entrepreneurship Theory and Practice*, 19 (1): 9–23.

Ireland, R. D., Covin, J. G., and Kuratko, D. F. (2009). Conceptualizing Corporate Entrepreneurship Strategy. *Entrepreneurship Theory and Practice*, 33 (1): 19–46.

Johannisson, B., Alexanderson, O., Nowicki, K., and Senneseth, K. (1994). Beyond Anarchy and Organization: Entrepreneurs in Contextual Networks. *Entrepreneurship and Regional Development*, 6 (3): 329–356.

Kets de Vries, M. F. R. (1993). The Dynamics of Family Controlled Firms: The Good News and the Bad News. *Organizational Dynamics*, 21 (3): 59–71.

Lambert, R. (2003). *Lambert Review of Business—University Collaboration*. London: HM Treasury.

Lansberg, I. (1999). *Succeeding Generations: Realizing the Dream of Families in Business*. Boston, MA: Harvard Business School Press.

Sharma, P. and Chrisman, J. J. (1999). Toward a Reconciliation of the Definitional Issues in the Field of Corporate Entrepreneurship. *Entrepreneurship Theory and Practice*, 23 (3): 11–27.

Vohora, A., Wright, M., and Lockett, A. (2004). Critical Junctures in the Growth in University High-Tech Spinout Companies. *Research Policy*, 33 (1): 147–175.

Westhead, P. (1997). Ambitions, 'External' Environment and Strategic Factor Differences between Family and Non-Family Companies. *Entrepreneurship and Regional Development*, 9 (2): 127–157.

Westhead, P. and Cowling, M. (1997). Performance Contrasts Between Family and Non-Family Unquoted Companies in the UK. *International Journal of Entrepreneurial Behaviour & Research*, 3 (1): 30–52.

Westhead, P., Cowling, M., and Howorth, C. (2001). The Development of Family Companies: Management and Ownership Issues. *Family Business Review*, 14 (4): 369–385.

Westhead, P. and Howorth, C. (2007). 'Types' of Private Family Firms: An Exploratory Conceptual and Empirical Analysis. *Entrepreneurship and Regional Development*, 19 (5): 405–431.

Wright, M., Hoskisson, R., Busenitz, L. and Dial, J. (2000). Entrepreneurial Growth through Privatization: The Upside of Management Buy-outs. *Academy of Management Review*, 25 (3): 591–601.

Wright, M, Clarysse, B., Mustar, P. and Lockett, A. (2007). *Academic Entrepreneurship in Europe*. Cheltenham: Edward Elgar.

Zahra, S., Gedajlovic, E., Neubaum, D., and Shulman, J. (2009). A Typology of Social Entrepreneurs: Motives, Search Processes and Ethical Challenges. *Journal of Business Venturing*, 24 (5): 519–532.

Chapter 7: The future

Anokhin, S. and Schulze, W. S. (2008). Entrepreneurship, Innovation, and Corruption. *Journal of Business Venturing*, 24 (5): 465–476.

Baumol, W. J. (1990). Entrepreneurship: Productive, Unproductive and Destructive. *Journal of Political Economy*, 98 (3): 893–921.

Beaver, G. and Jennings, P. (2005). Competitive Advantage and Entrepreneurial Power: The Dark Side of Entrepreneurship. *Journal of Small Business and Enterprise Development*, 12 (1): 9–23.

Birley, S. and Westhead, P. (1990). Growth and Performance Contrasts Between 'Types' of Small Firms. *Strategic Management Journal*, 11 (7): 535–557.

Davidsson, P., Delmar, F., and Wiklund, J. (2006). *Entrepreneurship and the Growth of Firms*. Cheltenham, UK: Edward Elgar.

Gill, K. (2010). *Of Poverty and Plastic: Scavenging and Scrap Trading Entrepreneurs in India's Urban Informal Economy*. New York: Oxford University Press.

Hayward, M., Shepherd, D., and Griffin, D. (2006). A Hubris Theory of Entrepreneurship. *Management Science*, 52 (2): 160–172.

Hoskisson, R., Wright, M., Filatotchev, I., and Peng, M. (2013). Emerging Multinationals from Mid-Range Economies: The Influence of Institutions and Factor Markets, *Journal of Management Studies*, forthcoming.

Kets de Vries, M. F. R. (1985). The Dark Side of Entrepreneurship. *Harvard Business Review*, 85 (6): 160–167.

Khavul, S., Bruton, G. D., and Wood, E. (2009). Informal Family Business in Africa. *Entrepreneurship Theory and Practice*, 33 (6): 1219–1238.

Mair, J. and Marti, I. (2009). Entrepreneurship In and Around Institutional Voids: A Case Study from Bangladesh. *Journal of Business Venturing*, 24 (5): 419–435.

Naude, W. (2010). *Promoting Entrepreneurship in Developing Countries: Policy Challenges*. Helsinki, Finland: United Nations University.

Osbourne, R. L. (1991). The Dark Side of Entrepreneur. *Long Range Planning*, 24 (3): 26–31.

Shepherd, D. (2003). Learning from Business Failure: Propositions about the Grief Recovery Process for the Self-Employed. *Academy of Management Review*, 28 (2): 318–329.

Storey, D. J. (1994). *Understanding the Small Business Sector*. London: Thomson Learning.

Ucbasaran, D., Alsos, G. A., Westhead, P., and Wright, M. (2008). Habitual Entrepreneurs. *Foundations and Trends® in Entrepreneurship*, 4 (4): 309–449.

Webb, J. W., Tihanyi, L., Ireland, R. D., and Sirmon, D. (2009). 'You Say Illegal, I Say Legitimate: Entrepreneurship in the Informal Economy'. *Academy of Management Review*, 34 (3): 492–510.

Webb, J. W., Bruton, G. D., Tihanyi, L., and Ireland, R. D. (2012). Research on Entrepreneurship in the Informal Economy: Framing a Research Agenda. *Journal of Business Venturing*, 28(5): 598–614.

Winslow, E. K. and Solomon, G. T. (1987). Entrepreneurs are More than Non-Conformist: They are Mildly Sociopathic. *Journal of Creative Behaviour*, 21 (3): 202–213.

Zahra, S. and Wright, M. (2011). Entrepreneurship's Next Act. *Academy of Management Perspectives*, 25: 67–83.

Permission to use a figure from the GEM 2011 Global Report has been granted by the copyright holders. The GEM is an international consortium and this report was produced from data collected in, and received from, 55 countries in 2011. Our thanks go to the authors, national teams, researchers, funding bodies and others contributors who have made this possible.

Index

A

academic spin-offs 48, 114–21
Academy of Management
    Entrepreneurship Division 3
achievement, need for (Nach) 80,
    81–3
adaptation 37
adjustment 89
affordable loss principle 35
agreeableness 81
Ajzen, Icek 84
ambiguity, tolerance for 80, 83
anchoring 89
arbitrage 25, 26
assistance policies 16–20, 75–8
Austin Reed Group 28
Austrian tradition 26
availability 89

B

background of entrepreneurs
    58–59, 63, 86–7
Bandura, Albert 92
Bangladesh, poverty reduction 131
Barbour, John 102–3
Barnes Family Entrepreneurship
    Bootcamp for Veterans with
    Disabilities 130

Barney, Jay 43
Baron, Robert 87–8
barriers to enterprise 12–13, 14–16
    for women 70–1
Baumol, William 129, 134
Becker, Gary 59
Beijing Science and Culture Book
    Information Corporation 30
benefits to entrepreneurs 49–50, 75
bird-in-the-hand principle 34
Birdseye, Clarence 21–2
blind spots 90
Branson, Richard 2
bricolage 35–7
bureaucracy 135
Busenitz, Lowell and Jay
    Barney 88
business failures, experience
    from 91, 95–7
business models 51–3
business plans 50–2
busted tech buyouts 113
buy-in/buyouts (BIMBOs) 110
buyouts 65, 109–14
    failures 111, 113

C

Cantillon, Richard 25
capabilities 46

capital resources 40–1, 46
  new types 132–3
causation approach 31–3
Central Surrey Health 124
Challenging the Frontiers of
    Poverty Reduction
    (CFPR) 131
charities 19
  as social enterprises 122–4
Chen, Jane 123
Chicago tradition 22–3
Classics tradition 26
cognitive theory 87–90, 127
commitment, entrepreneurial 120
comparative optimism 88, 90–1
competencies 46
conformation bias 89
conscientiousness 80, 84
context 128–9
control
  illusion of 89
  locus of 80, 83–4, 92
conventional roles of women 74
cooperatives 121
copyrights 49
corporate entrepreneurship
    (CE) 105–9
corporate venturing 106–7
cousin consortium family
    firms 104
Covin, John and Morgan Miles 107
craftsman entrepreneurs 63
crazy quilt principle 35
creation theory 27, 33–7, 41
creative destruction cycle 24
credibility 120

D

Dangdang.com 30
Darenote Limited 72
definition of 'entrepreneur' 4–6
denial 90
deviant personalities 86–7
direct corporate venturing 107

discovery theory 26–31, 33, 41
Divine Chocolate 124
domain redefinition 109
domestic roles of women 74
Dyson, James 2, 21

E

Eco-Lighthouse Foundation 124
economic benefits of
    entrepreneurship 1–2, 10–11,
    12–13
economic development 24
education in entrepreneurship 3–4
educational background 63
effectuation approach 32, 33–5,
    36–7
efficiency buyouts 110–11
Elahian, Kamran 95
Elvis and Kresse Organization
    (EaKo) 123–4
emotional stability 81, 84
entrepreneurial buyouts 111,
    112–13
entrepreneurial commitment 120
environmentally friendly firms 124
escalation of commitment 89
experience
  drawing on 94–5
  from failures 91, 95–7
exploitation of opportunities 38–9,
    42–9
external corporate venturing 106–7
external environment 8, 41–2
extraversion 81, 84

F

failures, experience from 91, 95–7
Fairburn, Mary 33
family firms 98–105
  buyouts 113–14
female entrepreneurs 67–75, 76
Ferguson, Mark 39
Fiet, Jim 29

finance 39–40, 42, 44, 75–8
  applying for 50–3
  new types 132–3
Forbes magazine 123
French etymology 4–5
French tradition 25–6
Freud, Sigmund 85
funding for entrepreneurs 2

G

Gartner, Bill 8, 85
Gates, Bill 2–3
gender stereotypes 67–8, 74
general human capital 59 *see also*
  human capital
Gibb, Allan and John Ritchie 55, 57–8
Global Entrepreneurship Monitor
  (GEM) studies 1, 61
goals of entrepreneurship,
  transformations 129
Goffee, Robert and Richard Scase 74
Goldman, Sam and Ned Tozun 123
government policies 16–20
Green-Works 124
growth of firms 125–8

H

habitual entrepreneurs 64–7, 77,
  91, 93–7
Haji-Ioannou, Stelios 2
Hammargren, Mai-Li 23
Hao Zhao 84
heuristics 88–90, 94, 112
Hill Holt Wood 124
Hitt, Mike 44
hubris 90
human capital 41, 44, 59–61

I

Illinois Investment Company
  Limited 28–9
illusion of control 89

imitation from competitors 49
India 132
informal entrepreneurs 135
innovation 2–3, 11, 21–2, 23–5, 28
  continuing 99
innovative women 74
input–process–output model 44–5
intellectual property (IP) 114–15,
  120–1
internal corporate venturing 106,
  107
International Finance
  Corporation 16–18
internationalization 48
intervention policies 16–20, 75–8
intrinsic motivation 89, 92
investor-led buyouts (IBOs) 109

J

Jobs, Steve 2–3

K

Kassalow, Jordan 123
Kenya Entrepreneurship
  Empowerment Foundation
  (KEEF) 130–1
Kets de Vries, Manfred 85–6, 101
Kirzner, Israel 26, 29–30, 31
Knight, Frank 22–3
Kohl's 112

L

law of small numbers 90
leadership style 86
lemonade principle 35
leveraged buyouts (LBOs) 109
Li Guoqing 30
liabilities of newness 15–16
lifestyle spin-offs 117–18, 119
Linn 99
local development 13
locus of control 80, 83–4, 92

M

MacMillan, Ian 63
management buy-ins (MBIs) 65, 110, 114
management buyouts (MBOs) 65, 109–14
market strategies 121
market transformations 2–3, 24
Marshall, Alfred 42
McClelland, David 81
microfinance 133
migrant workers 133
military servicemen, initiatives for 130
Million Dollar Homepage 3–4
Minogue, Kylie 72
monopoly profits 29
motivation, intrinsic 89, 92
motivation index 82–3
munificence 41
Mutewatch company 23

N

national-level promotion of entrepreneurship 129
need for achievement (Nach) 80, 81–3
negative effects of entrepreneurship 134–6
new firms 59–61, 62
newness
    liabilities 15–16
    as a strategy 47–8
new-technology-based firms (NTBFs) 51, 114, 115
Nine Dragons Paper Holdings 72–3
novice entrepreneurs 64, 77, 93

O

openness to experience 80, 84
opportunist entrepreneurs 63

opportunities
    creation 27, 33–7, 41
    discovery 26–31, 33, 41
    exploitation 38–9, 42–9
    recognition 119
optimism 88, 89, 90–1
orchestration of resources 46–9
Organisation for Economic Co-operation and Development (OECD) 5
outcomes 10
overconfidence 89

P

Paradigm Project, The 123
parents
    psychodynamic approach 86–7
    as role models 58
patents 49
personality traits 79–97
personality types 7, 10, 54–9, 61–3
    women 74
physical capital 40
pilot in the plane principle 35
planning fallacy 89
Poland 132
policy interventions 16–20, 75–8
portfolio entrepreneurs 64, 66, 77, 91
poverty, initiatives to combat 130–2
Prince's Trust Enterprise Programme 19
prior business ownership experience (PBOE) 64, 67, 77, 90–1, 93–7
private equity (PE) firms 109, 111, 113
process of entrepreneurship 6–8, 10
professional cousin consortium family firms 104
profits 25
prospector spin-offs 116–19

psychodynamics 85–7
psychological capital 41
public perception of
    entrepreneurs 2

R

radical innovation 24 *see also*
    innovation
radical women 74
Reed, Austin 28
regeneration 107
relationships, impact on 135–6
Renovo 39, 40, 115
representativeness 89
resources 38, 39–49, 59, 135
revitalization buyouts 111, 112
Reynolds, Paul 16, 59–61
risk-bearing 23
risk-taking 22–3, 79–81
Ritzén Praglowski, Oscar 23
Rotter, Julian 83
Roy, Marie Louise 69

S

Sarasvathy, Saras 31
Say, Jean-Baptiste 26
Schumpeter, Joseph 1–2, 23–5
Seagate Technology 113
self-efficacy, perceived 90, 92–3
serial entrepreneurs 64, 66, 77
Shackle, Len 23
Shane, Scott and Sankaran
    Venkataraman 30–1
Sharma, P. and J. J. Chrisman
    106
Shepherd, Dean 96
Shi Xiaoyang 28–9
Skazy, Tom 123
Smith, Norman 63
social benefits of
    entrepreneurship 13–14
social capital 41, 44
social context 54–8, 61–78

social development perspective 55,
    57–8
social enterprises 121–4, 129–30
socio-economic background 58
specific human capital 59 *see also*
    human capital
spin-off firms 48–9
    academic 114–21
Sseko Designs 123
Storey, David 18
strategic entrepreneurship
    (SE) 43–5
strategic renewal 105, 106,
    107–9
strategies 47–9
success syndrome 90
succession planning 102
support for entrepreneurs 16–20,
    75–8
sustainable returns 120
sustained regeneration 107

T

technological capital 40, 44
technology, new 21–2
television shows 3
temporal dimension 128
Tew, Alex 3–4
Thailand 132
themes 8–10
theory of planned behaviour 84–5
transitional family firms 104–5
types of entrepreneur 7, 10
types of organization 10

U

uncertainty 22–3, 25, 33
United Kingdom, social
    enterprises 123–4
United States
    initiatives for war
        veterans 130
    social enterprises 123

universities, academic
spin-offs 114–21
university courses 3–4

V

venture capital (VC) firms 2, 39, 50–1
backing spin-offs 116–18

W

Warburtons 99
Westhead, Paul 101

women as entrepreneurs
67–75, 76
Wright, Mike et al. 111, 116

Y

Yu Yu (Peggy Yu) 30

Z

Zhang Yin (Cheung Yan)
72–3
Zuckerberg, Mark 4, 22

ONLINE CATALOGUE
A Very Short Introduction

Our online catalogue is designed to make it easy to find your ideal Very Short Introduction. View the entire collection by subject area, watch author videos, read sample chapters, and download reading guides.

http://fds.oup.com/www.oup.co.uk/general/vsi/index.html

SOCIAL MEDIA
Very Short Introduction

Join our community
www.oup.com/vsi

- Join us online at the official Very Short Introductions **Facebook** page.
- Access the thoughts and musings of our authors with our online **blog**.
- Sign up for our monthly **e-newsletter** to receive information on all new titles publishing that month.
- Browse the full range of Very Short Introductions online.
- Read **extracts** from the Introductions for free.
- Visit our library of **Reading Guides**. These guides, written by our expert authors will help you to question again, why you think what you think.
- If you are a teacher or lecturer you can order inspection copies quickly and simply via our website.

Visit the Very Short Introductions website to access all this and more for free.
www.oup.com/vsi

LEADERSHIP
A Very Short Introduction
Keith Grint

In this *Very Short Introduction* Keith Grint prompts the reader to rethink their understanding of what leadership is. He examines the way leadership has evolved from its earliest manifestations in ancient societies, highlighting the beginnings of leadership writings through Plato, Sun Tzu, Machiavelli and others, to consider the role of the social, economic, and political context undermining particular modes of leadership. Exploring the idea that leaders cannot exist without followers, and recognising that we all have diverse experiences and assumptions of leadership, Grint looks at the practice of management, its history, future, and influence on all aspects of society.

ORGANIZATIONS
A Very Short Introduction
Mary Jo Hatch

This *Very Short Introductions* addresses all of these questions
and considers many more. Mary Jo Hatch introduces the
concept of organizations by presenting definitions and ideas
drawn from the a variety of subject areas including the physical
sciences, economics, sociology, psychology, anthropology,

al

Atlanta-Fulton Public Library